SUPER SIMPLE
QUICK START GUIDE TO
SELF-PUBLISHING

ALSO BY E.J. STEVENS

Super Simple Guides

Super Simple Quick Start Guide to Self-Publishing
Super Simple Quick Start Guide to Book Marketing

**Spirit Guide
Young Adult Series**

She Smells the Dead
Spirit Storm
Legend of Witchtrot Road
Brush with Death
The Pirate Curse

**Ivy Granger
Urban Fantasy Series**

Shadow Sight
Blood and Mistletoe
Ghost Light
Club Nexus
Burning Bright
Birthright
Hound's Bite
Blood Rite (Coming 2017)
Tales from Harborsmouth (Coming 2017)

**Hunters' Guild
Urban Fantasy Series**

Hunting in Bruges

Dark Poetry Collections

From the Shadows
Shadows of Myth and Legend

SUPER SIMPLE
QUICK START GUIDE TO
SELF-PUBLISHING

E.J. Stevens

Super Simple Quick Start Guide to Self-Publishing
Published by Sacred Oaks Press
Sacred Oaks, 221 Sacred Oaks Lane, Wells, Maine 04090

First Printing (trade paperback edition), January 2017

Copyright © E.J. Stevens 2016
All rights reserved

Stevens, E.J.
Super Simple Quick Start Guide to Self-Publishing / E.J. Stevens

ISBN 978-1-9460460-2-4 (trade pbk.)

PUBLISHER'S NOTE
This is a work of fiction. Names, characters, places, and incidents either are the product of the author's imagination or are used fictitiously, and any resemblance to actual persons, living or dead, business establishments, events, or locales is entirely coincidental.

The scanning, uploading and distribution of this book via the Internet or via any other means without the permission of the publisher is illegal and punishable by law. Please purchase only authorized electronic editions, and do not participate in or encourage electronic piracy of copyrighted materials. Your support of the author's rights is appreciated.

CONTENTS

Introduction	1
1: Build a Writing Template	5
2: Copyright	9
3: Beta Readers and Editors	14
4: ISBN and Barcodes	21
5: Font Licensing	27
6: Book Covers	31
7: ARCs	39
8: Ebook Formatting	49
9: Print Book Formatting	57
10: SEO, Keywords, and BISAC	67
11: Retail Product Pages	75
12: Pricing	85
13: Audiobook and Narrators	89
14: Translations and Translators	95
Publishing Checklist	101
Publishing Resources	103

INTRODUCTION

Welcome to the Super Simple Quick Start Guide to Self-Publishing. Whether novice or experienced writer, I hope you find this book helpful as you embark on your publishing journey. My goal is to provide you with an easy-to-follow guide that will save you time and money through tips and tricks I've developed during my writing career.

This guide is arranged in the order in which I publish my own books. Each chapter will take you one step, leap, or bound closer to successfully publishing your book. Early chapters introduce concepts vital to getting your book published, and give a simple tutorial on how to complete that step, saving you valuable time. Pro tips and publishing life hacks will highlight ways to avoid common pitfalls. Later chapters provide information on what to do after your book launch, including how to make your book available in additional languages and in the increasingly popular audiobook format. At the end of this guide, you'll also find a publishing checklist and a list of useful resources.

I have successfully published 15 fiction books, including the award-winning Spirit Guide young adult series, the bestselling Hunters' Guild urban fantasy series, and the award-winning, bestselling Ivy Granger, Psychic Detective urban fantasy series. In 2017, I will release my first works of nonfiction, the Super Simple Quick Start Guide to Book Marketing and this Super Simple Quick Start Guide to Self-Publishing. In addition to my 2017 nonfiction releases, I will be publishing two more books in the Ivy Granger series and two books in the much anticipated Whitechapel Paranormal Society Victorian Gothic horror series.

In recent years, my books have won numerous awards. I am a BTS Magazine Red Carpet Award winner for Best Novel and Best Book Cover, SYAE finalist for Best Paranormal Series, Best Novella, and Best Horror, winner of the PRG Reviewer's Choice Award for Best Paranormal Fantasy Novel,

Best Young Adult Paranormal Series, Best Urban Fantasy Novel, and finalist for Best Young Adult Paranormal Novel and Best Urban Fantasy Series.

My novels and novellas have been translated into multiple languages, including German, Italian, Spanish, and Dutch. I have also had the pleasure of working with world famous voice artists in the production of over a half dozen audiobooks.

My books have flown to the top of the Amazon bestsellers lists in numerous categories. I have repeatedly hit the Amazon top 100, and have hit #1 in a variety of categories such as the Mythology & Folktales > Fairy Tales category and the Mystery, Thriller & Suspense > Psychics category in Amazon stores worldwide.

I am a guest at conventions and book signings around the world. Recent conventions include Dragon Con, Boskone, Imaginarium, Readercon, and World Fantasy. I frequently speak on panels and teach workshops on a wide range of publishing, writing craft, and literary topics. I have been a guest speaker alongside such notable figures as Charles Stross, Catherynne M. Valente, Orson Scott Card, Rachel Vincent, Paul Tremblay, Maria Snyder, Leanna Renee Hieber, David Coe, Kit Reed, Peter V. Brett, Jacqueline Carey, and Max Gladstone.

It's important to remember that I did not start out as a publishing hero. I've made mistakes, ones that you don't have to make if you follow the steps in this guide.

When I started publishing my books in 2009, there were limited resources in libraries and online. I was frustrated by conflicting information, outdated books and websites, dead links leading to 404 errors, and false information posted by people with no industry experience.

Today there are hundreds of books, videos, and websites on how to publish and market your book. This wealth of resources is great in theory, but it means that it has become more difficult to find useful information than ever before. With my years of publishing experience, I can shine a light on the most important tasks, help you set clear goals, and provide tips to ensure you achieve those goals.

The Super Simple Quick Start Guide to Self-Publishing will give you the basic information needed to independently publish your book, while providing terminology and resources that will help if you wish to learn more advanced publishing skills.

Grab your cape. It's time to be a publishing hero!

CHAPTER 1: BUILD A WRITING TEMPLATE

If you haven't written your book yet, or you have more writing projects in the future, you will want to build a template that will make book formatting easier if you plan to publish your book in both ebook and print book formats. This template can be saved and reused each time you begin a new work. Setting up your document with these basic parameters will save you from hours of fixing formatting problems, which means you will have more time for writing and promoting your next book.

The writing template and tips in this chapter will help you avoid frustrating, time consuming pitfalls. Once you build your template, you can save it and use it for all future publishing projects. It will give you a good foundation, but remember that this template is not for publishing direct to ebook or print. Additional formatting is needed for both, and a tutorial on how to finish formatting will be presented in the chapters on ebook formatting and print formatting.

In the HOW TO section below, I provide a step-by-step tutorial on how to create a writing template in Microsoft Word. If you are using a different word processing program, go into the settings for that program and apply the following indent, font style, font size, and line spacing information. If you are using Microsoft Word, the HOW TO section in this chapter will walk you through how to change each setting.

Remember to save your template under a file name that is different from your current book project. This will make finding the template easier in the future. Once you have the template saved, you won't need to do this step again. Just open the Book Template file and start writing.

Writing Template Settings:
- Page Layout 8.5" x 11"

- Margins 1"
- Font Style Times New Roman
- Font Size 12pt
- Left Alignment
- First Line Indent 0.5"
- Line Spacing Single

Using the template is easy. The paragraph indent is already programmed as part of this template. If you look at the paragraph setting, it says First Line 0.5. That's what gives the paragraph its indent. Do not use the tab key or space bar to create an indent.

The normal style for this document is Times New Roman, 12pt font, single spaced, not bold or italic.

Later, when the book is done and you're ready for ebook or print book formatting, you'll add in your chapter headings. I'll show you a cool trick for formatting your headings using the Heading tool in Microsoft Word.

If you want to make something **bold** or *italic* while writing, go ahead. It won't mess up the normal template. Just don't worry about formatting the chapter headings. That's done later and is specific to the format, ebook or print.

I add one extra paragraph return when I come to the end of a chapter. Do not hit enter more than twice at any point in your document. You don't want excessive paragraph returns inside an ebook. It will cause weird things to happen, sometimes inserting large, random spaces and blank pages into your book.

If you need to add photos, do not copy and paste into your word processing document. Instead, use the **Insert** option and select **Picture**. Note that not everything under the **Insert** tab is supported in ebooks. Do not insert tables, headers, footers, or page numbers. Ebooks also do not support automatic formatting for bulleted lists and numbered lists. Do not use the **Bullets** and **Numbering** buttons to insert lists into your document.

You also never want to hit the tab key in this document. I will show you how to find and remove tabs in the chapter on ebook formatting, but it's best to get in the habit of not using the tab key. If you do use the tab key, the tab spacing will need to be removed later, creating more work for you or your formatter.

PRO TIP: NO tabs, NO headers or footers, and NO page numbers.

Note: The tutorial below uses Word 2010 and Word 2013. If you are using a different version of Word or a different word processing program, the names and pathways to your settings will vary. Do not worry. Apply the writing template settings provided in the bulleted list above for your template.

HOW TO: To create your template, open a new document and name the file **Book Template**. When using this template to write your book, remember to save your work in progress under a different file name. This way you will not overwrite your template.

Under **Page Layout** set the size of the document to 8.5 x 11 with 1 inch margins.

WORD 2010 USERS: Now you need to set the **Normal Style** for this document. Go to the **Home** tab, **Styles**, and click on the tiny **arrow** in the bottom right corner below **Change Styles**. Select **Normal** style, click on drop down arrow, and select **Modify**.

Under **Modify Style** click on the **Format** button in the bottom left of the window and select **Font**. Set the normal font to Times New Roman, 12pt, left alignment. Click **OK**.

Under **Modify Style** click on the **Format** button in the bottom left of the window and select **Paragraph**. Set the **Alignment** to left. Set **Indentation** to Left 0, Right 0, **Special** First Line by 0.5 inches. Set the **Spacing** to before 0, after 0, and **Line Spacing** to single. Check the **don't add space between paragraphs of same style** box. Click **OK**.

Then select **Paragraph** again and click the **Default** button, so that anything added after a page break or section break will have the same Normal formatting. It will all be the Normal style we've set here.

WORD 2013 USERS: Now you need to set the **Normal Style** for this document. Go to the **Home** tab, **Styles**, and click on the tiny **arrow** in the bottom right corner. Select **Normal** style, click on drop down arrow, and select **Modify**.

Under **Modify Style** click on the **Format** button in the bottom left of the window and select **Font**. Set the normal font to Times New Roman, 12pt, left alignment. Click **OK**.

Under **Modify Style** click on the **Format** button in the bottom left of the window and select **Paragraph**. Set the **Alignment** to left. Set **Indentation** to Left 0, Right 0, **Special** First Line by 0.5 inches. Set the **Spacing** to before 0, after 0, and **Line Spacing** to single. Check the **don't add space between paragraphs of same style** box. Click **OK**.

PRO TIP: If you need to print out your manuscript for reading and editing, save a copy under a different file name and change the line spacing from single to double space. This will make it easier to write and see editing notes. We'll discuss more on editing in **Chapter 3: Beta Readers and Editors**.

CHAPTER 2: COPYRIGHT

You've finished writing the first draft of your book. Now it's time to think about copyright.

Technically, in countries adhering to the Berne Convention, once you complete and save your work in a time-stamped file the copyright is automatic. Many writing sites will recommend mailing a copy of your manuscript through the postal service and saving the sealed, postmarked envelope in a safe place. This will establish a "poor man's" copyright.

If you plan to sell your book online, you should consider registering for copyright. A "poor man's" copyright will not offer the kind of protection you need if you end up in a copyright dispute. I have known authors whose books were uploaded to Amazon by a second party under false pretenses. The authors had to provide proof of copyright to continue to sell their books, and to have the false seller removed. It is not a common problem, but this short step can save you hours of hassle, so why take the risk?

Copyright registration is cheap and easy, especially if you apply before your book is published (see this chapter's PRO TIP for more details). A standard copyright registration for a single author work in the United States costs just $35, though an expedited application can cost much more.

I prefer to apply for copyright registration before sending my manuscript off to beta readers, editors, and reviewers. This way I have an application date and confirmation number issued before the manuscript is ever shared to prove that I am the original creator of the literary work and I have the exclusive rights for its use and distribution.

Visit your country's copyright office online to apply. In the U.S., visit the United States Copyright Office online (copyright.gov). A step-by-step tutorial on how to apply with the United States Copyright Office is provided in this chapter's HOW TO section below.

HOW TO: Visit the United States Copyright Office website at **copyright.gov**. Note that the steps here are based on the copyright registration form in place as of December 2016. Click the **Help** link at the top right of the page for the Copyright Office's help page if you have any trouble.

Scroll down to **Register a Copyright**. If your privacy and security settings are blocking this option, use the **Search** box to search for eCO Registration System. Click **Log in to eCO** (Electronic Copyright Office) and enter your username and password or create a new account. From the left sidebar, select **Register New Claim.**

Click the box to answer the three yes or no questions. If registering a novel with one author, the answer will be yes to all. If you answer with a no, a warning will pop up with instructions. If you answer yes to all three questions, you can click the blue **Start Registration** button.

Select a **Type of Work,** such as **Literary Work,** from the drop down list. Click on each type of work for a description. Click the box to confirm you understand the description. On each screen you can select **Continue** when you've completed that screen's form or **Save for Later** to save the application as a working case in your dashboard. For the sake of this tutorial, we'll click **Continue** to advance to the next page of the application.

Click the **New** button. Select the **Title Type,** such as **Title of Work Being Registered,** from the drop down list. Enter the **Title of This Work**. Click the **Continue** button to save and go to the next page.

Select yes or no from the **Has This Work Been Published** drop down list. **Enter Year of Completion**. If you answered yes, you will need to enter information on nation and year of publication. Click the **Continue** button to save and go to the next page.

Name the author of the work being registered. If you are the author, click the blue **Add Me** button.

Give either an **Individual Author Name** or **Organization Name**, but not both. Select either **Citizenship** or **Domicile**, but not both.

Check the box to indicate the **Author's Contribution**. This is normally **Text**.

If you are the only author, click **Continue** to save and continue. If there are multiple authors, click **New** to add another author and follow the instructions above.

Identify the claimant. That is normally you. If you are the claimant, click the blue **Add Me** button. Claimant's name can be either an **Individual Author Name** or **Organization Name**, but not both. If any claimant is not an author, select the transfer statement option. When you are done entering claimants, click the **Continue** button to save and go to the next page.

You only need to fill out the next screen if you wish to limit your claim. Only check off items to be excluded from your claim. Otherwise, leave this screen blank. Click the **Continue** button to save and go to the next page.

Provide a rights and permissions contact. If you would like to be the rights and permissions contact, click the blue **Add Me** button. If you wish to designate an agent authorized to grant permission to use your work, fill in their name and contact information. Click the **Continue** button to save and go to the next page.

Provide a correspondent contact. If you would like to be the correspondent contact, click the blue **Add Me** button. If you would prefer someone else be contacted with questions regarding your application, fill in their name and contact information. Click the **Continue** button to save and go to the next page.

Provide a name and address to mail your copyright registration certificate to. If you would like to be the correspondent contact, click the blue **Add Me** button. Click the **Continue** button to save and go to the next page.

Only fill out the next screen if you have a compelling reason for expedited processing. This is an expensive option! The special handling fee is $800. Otherwise, leave this screen blank. Click the **Continue** button to save and go to the next page.

Enter the **Name of the Certifying Individual** and check the box indicating that you are the author, copyright claimant, owner of exclusive rights, or their authorized agent. Click the **Continue** button to save and go to the next page.

If your application is ready to send, all categories will have a checkmark in the left sidebar. Carefully review your application information. If complete, click the blue **Add to Cart** button.

Click the blue **Checkout** button for payment. Click the blue **Pay Credit Card/ACH** button to pay with credit card or electronic funds transfer.

Option 1 is **Electronic Funds Transfer**. Scroll down past this section if you wish to pay with a credit card.

Option 2 is **Credit Card**.

Fill in payment information for Option 1 or 2 and click the **Continue with ACH** button or the **Continue with Plastic Card Payment** button.

Enter your email address. Check the box to authorize the charge. Click the **Submit Payment** button.

Payment successful should show at the top of the screen. Now you need to send a copy of your work to complete the submission process. Click the blue **Continue** button to submit a copy of your work.

You must upload your work online or send by mail, not both.

ELECTRONIC SUBMISSION: Works that are unpublished or have not been published in print can be uploaded electronically. Read the acceptable file size and file type requirements in blue. Click the green **Select Files to Upload** button and find your file. Make sure the file name is correct. Remove any incorrect files. Click the blue **Start Upload** button. When all files are uploaded, click the green **Click Here to Complete Your Submission After Uploading All Files** button.

You will receive a confirmation email. **Save and print** this for your records. Click the **Home** tab to visit your dashboard. Your cases will be listed on the dashboard screen. Select **Search My Cases** in the left sidebar to view a printable copy of your application.

SNAIL MAIL SUBMISSION: When submitting a hard copy of your book, you must first complete the application and payment electronically. On the **Payment Confirmation** screen, click the **Submit Your Work** button, and click the **Send by Mail** link. Click the **Shipping Slip** link to create a shipping slip to be attached to your work.

PRO TIP: Apply for copyright registration before publishing your book. If your book has been published in print, you will be required to mail copies to the copyright office. Your application will take longer to process, and you will need to spend additional money on books and shipping costs.

CHAPTER 3:
BETA READERS AND EDITORS

Every book needs professional editing. The rate an editor will charge depends on multiple factors, including length, how rough the manuscript is, and how fast you need the work completed. This is why beta readers have the potential to save you money. Beta readers will help you turn in a more polished manuscript that will require less work and take less time to edit.

Beta Readers:
Beta readers are fans or writers who are willing to read a rough, early draft of your manuscript and provide constructive criticism. Beta readers commonly give feedback on whether a scene is confusing, if words or information are missing, consistency errors, and basic grammatical errors. This is usually done free of charge, although some beta readers are now charging a small fee.

With the popularity and ease of electronic readers, more beta readers and reviewers are requesting books, even rough manuscripts, in formats compatible with reading apps and portable reading devices. If you want to keep your beta readers happy, offer your manuscript in a choice of .doc/.docx (Word), PDF, and mobi (Kindle). Tutorials on how to convert your files to these formats can be found in the chapter on ARCs (the easy, quick and dirty way) and in the chapter on Ebook Formatting.

For beta readers, I use the same method that I use when providing multiple format options of ARCs for reviewers. But it is important to remember beta readers are not reviewers. Feedback from beta readers is for you directly, not the general public. The only exception is if you wish to form a private discussion group where multiple beta readers can discuss your work. This can be done in a coffee shop, in a private Google+ chat circle, or a private Facebook group. Be sure to set clear rules, especially if creating a discussion group.

Also, keep your beta readers happy. Give them coffee, candy, and baked goods. Send them a thank you card, letter, or email. When your book is ready to publish, mention your beta readers in the acknowledgements, in a blog post or interview, and give them a signed copy of your book. Unlike reviewers, beta readers are not posting reviews to online retailers, so giving them gifts is not a violation of a retailer or distributor's terms of service. We'll cover more on avoiding the pitfalls of violating Amazon's TOS in later chapters.

Editors:

You've sent your manuscript to beta readers, and you now have a clean, well-written second, third, or fourth draft. Once your manuscript is free of obvious errors and plot holes, it becomes more and more difficult to spot problems. It's time to hire an editor.

An independent or freelance editor is someone who will read and edit your manuscript for structure, plot, style, continuity, and grammatical errors. Some editors or editing packages will offer different levels of editing with different areas of focus.

A **critique** will cover a basic overall assessment of your manuscript. The editor will point out your manuscript's strengths and weaknesses, but this type of editing will not provide you with detailed line editing.

Developmental editing, **content editing**, or **substantive editing** will point out structural problems, plot holes, underdeveloped characters, and poor pacing. This form of editing goes beyond a critique, and the editor will provide notes on suggested ways to fix the manuscript, or may rewrite some sections.

Copy editing includes checking for grammar, style, spelling, and punctuation problems.

Proofreading is a lighter form of editing that checks for typos, spelling, and punctuation errors. The term proofreading comes from the practice of editing a proof copy of the work after it has been edited, designed, and formatted. Although this isn't always the practice, it is a good idea to have an editor or skilled beta reader make a pass through your final, formatted ARCs for any errors that may have inadvertently been added during the formatting process.

Keep in mind that not all editors use the definitions above, or they might use a more flexible combination of these terms. Some editors will refer to their services or editorial packages as a light, medium, or heavy edit. Armed with the information above, ask specific questions about what their editing services include.

Where can you find an editor? There are many places that you can go to find a quality editor. Good places to start are forums frequented by professional writers such as the KBoards Writer's Café, local writer's groups, online writer's groups, and professional organizations such as HWA (Horror Writers Association) and SFWA (Science Fiction and Fantasy Writers of America). Professional organizations have great resources for members. These organizations allow both traditionally and independently published authors membership, but typically have a sales requirement for admission.

While searching for an editor, you will need to know how to spot frauds and unqualified editors. Be prepared to ask questions. What is their experience? What are their credentials, including what books and authors they have worked for? How long have they been editing?

A qualified editor should have a list of published books and articles that they have edited. They will have references available upon request. If an editor's references are not posted on their website, and verifiable, ask for them.

Editors should also be willing to provide a sample of their work. A sample will give you an idea of the quality of their work and what to expect from their paid services.

If in doubt, ask around and do a search on the individual or firm's name. You can also check sites like Writer Beware (writerbeware.com), the Writer Beware blog (accrispin.blogspot.com) and Preditors & Editors (pred-ed.com). These sites keep track of scams targeting writers.

Like all business contracts, make sure all details are covered and you get it in writing. It may be a good idea to have author friends look over the contract before signing. If information is vague or you're expected to accept a verbal promise of services, go elsewhere. Never assume that you're going to get something that is not expressed in writing.

Cost is another factor to consider when searching for an editor. The Editorial Freelancers Association (the-efa.org) in the U.S. and the Society for Editors and Proofreaders (sfep.org.uk) in the U.K. each have a chart on recommended rates for editorial services. This will give you a good idea of what to expect, but factors like how rough your manuscript is and the required turn-around time will have an impact on your editing expenses.

Just like with expedited shipping options, requiring an editor to work faster will cost more money. Also keep in mind that most quality editors will have a large client list. Unless they've had a cancellation, it is unlikely that an editor will be able to immediately work on your manuscript. Many editors will schedule manuscripts up to 3 months in advance, but editors in demand may be booked as far out as a year in advance. When working with publishing professionals such as editors, cover artists, and book formatters, be considerate of their workload and have realistic expectations of when work will be completed, or be willing to pay for the expedited services.

Once you have a contract date for when work is due from your editor, add it to your calendar. You will want to block off time to work on making corrections to your manuscript once you receive these edits. If this is your first book, you will likely need multiple rounds of editing.

If writing a lengthy book series, you may also want to consult with a dedicated consistency editor. This is another expense to budget for, and will need to be considered when setting a release date.

Not sure how long the editing process will take? If you have never worked with an editor, give yourself at least a month to work on editing. I also highly recommend adding a buffer for the unexpected. Authors and editors get sick, have family emergencies, and fall behind. If you plan for delays in the publishing process, you'll be less stressed when these things happen.

PRO TIP: Keep detailed notes on your characters and world building details while writing your book(s). Notes can easily be added to manuscripts in Scrivener, kept in a separate Word document, sorted in spreadsheets such as Excel, or added as an additional color of sticky note if you use a plot board. Detailed notes and attentive beta readers can save you from the expense of a consistency editor and/or from publishing a book with errors that may lead to angry readers and poor reviews. Readers have minds like a steel trap, and they will notice the change in a name, location, or a character's eye color.

CHAPTER 4: ISBN AND BARCODES

There are many options to consider when publishing your book. Whether or not you need to purchase ISBNs and barcodes will depend on factors such as what formats you intend to publish, what companies you choose for printing your books, and if you wish to produce the most professional book possible. If you decide to purchase your own ISBNs and barcodes, you can find detailed instructions in the HOW TO section below.

ISBN:

An International Standard Book Number (ISBN) is a unique number that identifies your book. An ISBN is required for the sale and distribution of any publication. Current ISBNs are 13 digits long. Using this 13 digit number, any distributor, retailer, library, or individual can locate your book.

Just remember that every edition of your book will require its own ISBN. A different ISBN is needed for each hardcover, trade paperback, mass market paperback, audio, and ebook editions.

Some print on demand (POD) companies have a free or reduced price ISBN option, but this usually lists the POD company as the publisher. For Amazon's Createspace it will list the book's publisher as Createspace Independent Publishing Platform. Similarly, if you purchase an ISBN under your personal name, you will be listed as the publisher. The most professional approach is to create a DBA (doing business as) name to publish under and purchase your ISBN with that name.

Note: For the purposes of this guide, I am referring to your DBA as the name you identify when purchasing your ISBN and the name that is listed on retail product pages as the name of your publisher. To take this a step further and legally register for a DBA with the government, you need to check your local and state regulations. Even within the U.S., the legal requirements vary hugely from state to state and county to county.

You will need a different ISBN for each print format. The cost of purchasing individual ISBNs can add up fast, so consider the larger ISBN package. If you plan to publish more than one book or in more than one format, the large ISBN package will save you money.

If publishing only one book, you can reduce your number of needed ISBNs by using the free ISBNs offered for your ebook editions. Ebook companies like Amazon KDP, Smashwords, Draft2Digital, and PubIt do not require that you own and provide an ISBN. A number can be assigned to your book for free. A similar option is available with some audiobook production companies and with companies that produce translated editions.

Knowing how many books you plan to publish, and the different formats you plan to publish, will help you decide on what ISBN package to purchase. As you can see in the list below, prices vary by package size and by your country of residence.

Purchasing ISBNs:
- Canada: Library and Archives (FREE)
- Australia: Thorpe-Bowker ($42-$3,035)
- United Kingdom: Nielson (£89-£949)
- United States: Bowker ($125-$1,500)

How ISBNs are issued is country specific. If your country is not listed here, you can find a comprehensive list at the International ISBN Agency's website (www.isbn-international.org/agencies). If you are a Canadian self-publisher, your ISBNs are 100% free at ISBN Canada online (www.bac-lac.gc.ca/) through the Library and Archives Canada government site. Sadly, providing free ISBNs is not the norm.

Most countries, including the United States, require that ISBNs be purchased through a private company. In Australia, ISBNs are purchased through Thorpe-Bowker (www.myidentifiers.com.au/). In the United Kingdom, ISBNs are purchased through Nielsen (www.nielsenisbnstore.com). In the United States, ISBNs are purchased through Bowker (www.myidentifiers.com). Detailed instructions for purchasing an ISBN in the United States can be found in this chapter's HOW TO section below.

Barcodes:
A barcode is necessary for the back of a print book's cover. The barcode typically encodes the ISBN and suggested retail price. Before purchasing a barcode, check the policies for your print company. Print on demand (POD) companies like Createspace will produce a barcode for your book for free.

If you decide to have your books printed by a private printer, or wish to use your own barcode with a POD company, you can purchase a barcode for your book online. Barcodes are usually offered as an additional item when purchasing your ISBNs. An exception is in Canada where information on how to procure a barcode is provided as a FAQ on the page where you acquire your free ISBN.

When using your own barcodes, you or your book cover designer will need to add the barcode to the back of the book. Barcode size and placement should be considered when designing your print book cover. Barcodes must be high resolution and are usually 2 inches wide by 1.2 inches tall. They almost always are black numbers and lines on a white rectangle to provide enough contrast to be scanned. When designing a wrap around book cover image, plan accordingly.

If using a free barcode from a POD company like Createspace, they will add the barcode to the bottom right corner of the back cover of your book. Make sure that no important cover elements, such as images or text, appear where the barcode will be printed.

HOW TO: If you are self-publishing from the United States, you will need to purchase your ISBNs and barcodes from **Bowker** at www.myidentifiers.com. Note that the steps here are based on the copyright registration form in place as of December 2016.

Click the **Buy Your ISBN Today** button. Choose the package that best suits your publishing needs. You can purchase 1 ISBN for $125, 10 ISBNs for $250-$295, 100 ISBNs for $575, or 1,000 ISBNs for $1,500. I highly recommend purchasing one of the medium or larger packages. At current rates, 10 ISBNs cost the same as purchasing 2 ISBNs individually.

Click the blue **Buy Now** button to add the package to your online shopping cart. A pop-up window will ask if you want to purchase a barcode. Add if needed.

Click on **View Cart**. You should see the items you want in your cart. Click remove to delete any items you do not want to purchase. When ready, click the green **Check Out** button.

Sign in or create a new account with Bowker. Complete payment information.

Make sure that your email address is correct. This is where your ISBN confirmation will be sent. Print out your confirmation for your records. The confirmation will also provide information on how to access your numbers and barcodes.

Using the link in the email confirmation, or by visiting the website directly, return to the Bowker site. Log in and click on your name in the upper right of the screen to access your Bowker account. This will bring you to your dashboard.

Click on the **My Identifiers** tab in your dashboard. You will see a list of all of the ISBNs that you purchased.

If the ISBN has not been used, a blue **Assign Title** button will show in the **Title** column. Keep in mind that although this page will update using information from online retailers, you are still responsible for keeping track of the ISBNs that you use.

For example, if you assign an ISBN to the trade paperback edition of a book months before its release and post that number on the book's Goodreads book page, the ISBN will still appear to be unused in the Bowker dashboard. Goodreads is not a retailer, so Bowker does not track ISBN use from the Goodreads site. I recommend keeping a spreadsheet dedicated to tracking your ISBN use.

In the **My Identifiers** section of your dashboard, you can manually upload the book's title and book cover, or let the system pull the information from retailers. I recommend uploading a higher resolution cover than the one that the system uses as default. This will provide a more appealing, professional listing in the Books in Print database.

PRO TIP: You can't transfer individual ownership of an ISBN. That means that a self-publisher can't change the publisher name after you purchase an ISBN. If purchasing a large package of ISBNs, remember that ALL of the ISBNs will have the same publisher name. This name does not have to be your personal name.

The name on the ISBN can't be changed, so the only way to change the publisher name on your book is to release a new edition with a new ISBN.

PRO TIP: You can't use a friend's ISBNs. Two or more authors can't purchase a large package of numbers and share them. The only way to share ISBNs is to form a small publishing business together and publish under the same imprint, which will add complications.

PRO TIP: If you are getting your publishing rights back from a publisher, you can't use the original ISBN. You will need to purchase new ISBNs for all formats of the book.

CHAPTER 5: FONT LICENSING

Whether you decide to hire someone to create your book covers (highly recommended) and interior book formatting or do the work yourself, it's time to think about your book design. An important element in book cover design and interior print book design is your title font.

The title font is the font that will be used on your book cover. Your cover fonts are also often used on the title page of your book's print edition.

Even when working with a high-end book cover designer, the choice of your title font is up to you. You can leave the decision in their capable hands, but it will sometimes cost more. Even if cost is not an issue, failing to choose and own the rights to your title font can have lasting ramifications.

Fonts are protected by copyright. Want to sell t-shirts, buttons, mugs, and tote bags using your cover image? Want to use your title font on banners, posters, and online advertisements? The safest way to do this is to choose and purchase the rights to your title font or to make sure that your font is a public domain font (meaning nobody owns rights to it) with no licensing restrictions for commercial use. Remember, as a writer, you are a business, and so you have to take into consideration commercial licensing. Even if you purchase a commercial font license, make sure that you understand any licensing restrictions such as limits to the number of printings.

This may take some research. Many download sites for fonts have confusing or inaccurate information about the font's commercial licensing. Use caution when downloading fonts from sites like Dafont (www.dafont.com) and Font Squirrel (www.fontsquirrel.com). These can be a good place to begin your search, but never use a font without clear license information. Find the contact information for the font's designer, sometimes included as a Read Me file with the font download, and contact them directly. There are also some great design companies that sell custom fonts.

Just like stock photos, the licenses for fonts, and their cost, can vary greatly. The average price that I've paid for a title or subtitle font is $75. If using the font for a series, the cost is spread out over all books in the series. You'll only need to buy the font once. Purchasing a commercial font license is an investment that can save you from anxiety, future frustration, and potential legal fees.

HOW TO: Look at covers in your genre to see what font styles are popular. Fonts are typically very specific to a genre. You'll see fancy elegant letters in high fantasy and sharp angular letters in military science fiction, so check carefully.

It will help to know that there are four basic types of font styles: serif, sans serif, script, and decorative. A serif font, such as Times New Roman, Century Schoolbook, and Garamond, has small lines or feet at the ends of each letter. Sans serif fonts, literally meaning without serif, do not have these lines. Sans serif fonts include Arial and Helvetica, and are also sometimes called Gothic or Roman fonts. Script fonts are based on the fluid, curving lines of cursive handwriting. Decorative fonts, sometimes called display fonts, usually have extreme features, are more artistic and eye-catching, and are best suited for headlines and titles. Decorative fonts should be used sparingly, and are not suitable for using in body text such as the blurb on your back cover.

Select your top 3 font choices for your title, subtitle, author name, and back cover blurb (if creating a wrap-around cover for print). At the time of writing this, the standard is sans serif for titles or larger text and serif for smaller text.

Now test the fonts. Even if you pick a font that looks great on a font site, make sure to test it on your cover before purchasing.

Bulk font sites will let you download the font at your own risk, leaving you to handle the licensing on your own. Design companies will have example fonts that you can download, or you can save the image of the font from your screen (right-click and save image) and insert it into your cover. It doesn't have to be a perfect, high resolution copy of the font for a mock-up. This is a draft to make sure that the font suits your overall cover design.

Once you find a font that suits your cover, download the font. You will receive a **ZIP File**. Open the zipped file, and inside the folder will be a document with the font, sometimes more than one variation of the font. There may also be a **Read Me** file with license information and the name of the font's creator.

To install the font that you want, double-click on the font file to **open** it and click the **Install** button. (If using a Mac OS, put the files into **/Library/Fonts**.) Your computer may require a **restart** before the font displays in your font options.

Now you can select your custom font from the font style drop down list in your word processing and cover design programs. You can also send the zipped file folder to your cover designer as an email file attachment.

Remember that even if you have hired a book cover designer to handle your book cover, you will need the font installed on your computer for adding to your print book's interior title page. Additional information on embedding fonts for print book publishing can be found in **Chapter 9: Print Book Formatting**.

PRO TIP: Keep a file with printed copies of all of your font and stock photo licenses for your books. Email confirmations on your laptop or phone are great, but can be difficult to find when you really need them.

CHAPTER 6: BOOK COVERS

Every book needs a professional looking book cover. This is true no matter which of the three ways to create a book cover—Custom, Premade, or Do-It-Yourself—you choose. Readers judge books by their covers.

The quality of your book cover will influence the assumptions a potential reader will make about your book. If it looks like no effort was put into your cover art and design, then readers will assume that no effort was put into the writing and interior formatting of your book. No matter how wonderful your book is, if the cover is terrible, it will not sell.

In addition to being high quality, your cover must be eye catching. A book cover is often a reader's first introduction to your book. With thousands of books for readers to choose from, you need to make your book stand out from the crowd.

A book's cover should also reflect your story's genre. Readers will be disappointed if they buy a book with a romance cover and the story inside is zombie horror. This doesn't mean that you can't deviate from the norm. You may want to try something new in an effort to stand out from the crowd. But be aware that certain objects, settings, behaviors, and font styles will influence what a reader will assume your book is about. For example, dragons indicate fantasy, biohazard symbols indicate post-apocalyptic zombie horror, and spaceships indicate science fiction.

If your book is a cozy mystery, artwork that includes a cat, a pie, and a poison bottle on a cottage windowsill with a rounded title font style will probably receive a better response from readers than a cover featuring a spaceship with a modern font.

As indie authors, we have the luxury of working outside any traditional publishing rules, but it is helpful to know what the rules are. Some rules exist for a reason. While bending the rules of cover design might work, it's worth considering the risks. A cover shouldn't confuse the reader. If the cover has nothing to do with your book, you run the risk of missing potential sales and of receiving bad reviews. Bad reviews can be the kiss of death to any book, especially independently published books.

My advice is to look at the book covers of successful books in your genre or subgenre. Amazon and Goodreads are great places to search for examples of print and ebook cover design. I like to begin a cover search on Goodreads using their Listopia feature. A detailed, step-by-step tutorial on using Listopia to search for book covers and create a reference file for you or your cover designer can be found in the HOW TO section below.

Once you have a folder of book covers from your genre for reference, you can begin narrowing down elements that are common to your genre and the elements that are most appealing to you. Is it the model, setting, title font, or color palette? Thinking about these things now will help you when designing your cover or working with a professional artist.

This is also a good time to be thinking about alternate formats. Do you plan to create an audiobook? If so, you can search Audible and iTunes for audiobook cover design ideas. Audio covers require a square, high resolution cover. If you want your book covers to match across formats, consider having a wide cover created that can be cropped for print and ebook. A narrow cover that works for print and ebook will need to be cropped at the top and bottom to work for audio. If important design elements are in these locations, they will be lost.

I discussed font licensing in the previous chapter. If you decide to let a professional cover designer create your book cover, pay to have them produce your cover for all formats, including audio. If you can't afford all formats, ask for the original Photoshop file and/or your cover in high resolution without the fonts. Be aware that receiving these files is dependent on your contract with your designer. You can get a cheaper design if the designer maintains rights to their intellectual property. Sometimes it will cost extra to get editable files.

The reason for getting a clean file without fonts is because a completed book cover that is created for a 6x9 trade paperback will not work for a square audiobook cover. Your fonts will also need to be updated for book covers of all translated editions. This is one of the reasons that I avoid premade book covers. Premade book covers are cheap, but lack the flexibility to be adapted to multiple formats. If you plan to publish in multiple formats, premade covers will cost you money for each format, losing their cost effectiveness.

Now that you have a folder of reference art, it's time to decide if you will pay a professional book cover designer for a custom cover, buy a premade cover, or do the work yourself.

Do-It-Yourself:

Do not create your own book covers unless you are an artist skilled in graphic design, you are willing to sit through weeks of workshops and tutorials, or you have a skilled friend who can help you. Keep in mind that being skilled at web design, logo design, and illustration doesn't necessarily mean you have the skills specific to book cover design. Even if you have experience with book cover design, your book is your baby. Just like with the need for beta readers and professional editors, you will need to get feedback on your covers before publishing.

Pitfalls to watch for are misspelled words, blurry low resolution images, illegible fonts, lack of contrast, and poor photo manipulation.

If you are still determined to do the work yourself, there are thousands of photos available for use online. Make sure that you read the details on the commercial use of photos. Most stock photo sites like DepositPhotos (depositphotos.com) and iStock Photo (istockphoto.com) have clear contracts. You will need to purchase the extended commercial license to use any image(s) on a book cover of a book that you are going to sell.

With a little creativity and luck, you might be able to create an inexpensive book cover on your own. I set out to create an easy, inexpensive, D.I.Y. cover for this Super Simple guide. I wanted to prove that, albeit risky, it is possible to create an attractive cover on a budget.

Here is the breakdown:

- Stock Photos $40
- Custom Font $16

The total cost for this D.I.Y. book cover was $56.

Premade Cover:

Premade covers vary in price depending on the artist, if the cover is being sold as an exclusive, and if it is tailored to ebook, print, or audio format.

Some premade covers are very low quality. Consider the pitfalls discussed above, like appearance and size, when choosing a premade cover. If you want an exclusive cover, make sure that you have it clearly stated in writing that the cover will not be sold or used again after purchase.

Ebook covers are typically the cheapest. The resolution and size are not always compatible for use in print, so you will not be able to use a premade ebook cover for a print cover later.

Premade print covers are the most expensive. Make sure to ask if you are getting a full wrap-around cover or just a high resolution front cover, and remember that wrap-around cover size will always need to be adjusted to your print book's trim size and spine width. Spine width is calculated by page count and paper thickness, so will be different for every book.

Audiobook covers will need to abide by the standards set by ACX, the company that most indie authors use for creating and distributing audiobooks. ACX requires a minimum size of 2400 x 2400 pixels, 72 dpi resolution, and images must be a true square.

Premade covers range in price from $25 to $250. Most premade ebook covers will cost around $65. Some sites will offer a discount if you are buying multiple covers for a series or multiple cover formats. Make sure that pricing, exclusivity, delivery method, size, and resolution are clearly stated.

Custom Cover:

Hiring a professional cover designer to create a customer book cover is expensive, but it is an investment into your book's future. A high quality, well-designed book cover will have a better chance of selling and earning you royalties.

Extremely well designed covers might also be eligible for book cover awards. Having any kind of award associated with your book helps to boost sales. The cover for my book *Birthright*, a novel in the Ivy Granger urban fantasy series, was nominated and received an honorable mention in the 2015 BTS Red Carpet Book Awards. This award helped to propel sales for the book and for the series.

Custom covers range in price from $150-$5,000. Most custom covers will cost around $500. Some artists will offer a discount to authors who are commissioning work on multiple covers. If you have a series planned, let the artist know. You can negotiate your contract to include future books which will help lower your price.

Hybrid Cover:
I recently updated the book cover for my urban fantasy novel, *Hunting in Bruges*. I collected a dozen covers as reference, found links to the stock photo images for the model and background, chose a color palette, and hired PhatPuppy Art Studios to do the photo manipulation and design for the cover art.

I prefer to handle the fonts myself, so our agreement was for the art only. I chose and purchased custom fonts and did the font placement. This is a hybrid of the custom cover and do-it-yourself methods. If using the hybrid method, make sure that your professional artist is clear on what work you expect them to complete and what work you will be responsible for.

Use the information in **Chapter 5: Font Licensing** when shopping for the fonts to use on your cover, and use contrasting sizes for your fonts. One element—the title, author name, or series name—needs to be larger than everything else. The largest element is most often the title or author name. Also, don't use more than three font styles on your front cover. When repeating a font style for more than one element, consider changing the color, size, or boldface.

Here is the breakdown for a hybrid cover:
- Professional Artist $300-$700
- Font License $100

If you have a book cover that you are unhappy with, you can hire a cover designer to create a new cover. Traditional publishers do this all the time. As indie publishers, we have the ability to quickly respond to reader feedback and lackluster sales. What might take a traditional publisher years to change, we can fix in 24-72 hours.

In the example of my book *Hunting in Bruges*, the novel was stuck at #200 in Vampire Horror on Amazon. After updating the book with a new cover and running a brief price promotion, the book jumped up to #11. Sales have continued to be better since updating the cover, so I consider the expense of experimenting with new covers a wise investment.

HOW TO: Create a new folder named **Book Cover Reference** by right clicking, selecting **New**, **Folder**, and typing the name of your new folder. This is where you will save the book covers that you like most in your book's genre.

Note that once again, these instructions are for a PC. For a Mac, the instructions will be similar, but not exactly the same.

Now we want to use the **Listopia** feature on Goodreads to search for the top reader picks in our book's genre. Go to **Goodreads** (www.goodreads.com) and sign in or create an account.

Go to the **Browse** tab, and select **Lists** from the drop down menu. In the **Search Lists** field in the upper right, enter the genre or subgenre of your book and click the **Search** button.

Try to be as specific as possible. For example, if your book is urban fantasy, a search for urban fantasy will provide more accurate results than a broader search of fantasy.

Scroll down through the lists and look at trends. Right click and **Save** the book cover images that you like into your **Book Cover Reference** folder.

Note: There are many color specific lists on Listopia. If you are attracted to a color palette for your book's cover and want to see more examples, you can search Listopia for popular book covers with that color. For example, in the **Search Lists** field type the words **Blue Covers** and click the **Search** button. There are 45 lists of books with blue covers on Listopia.

The most popular lists featuring the most books and with the most reader votes will appear at the top of the page.

In the case of our search for books with blue covers, the most popular Listopia list features 2,696 books with 849 voters.

You can expand your search to sites like Amazon, Library Thing, and Book Likes, but I find the Listopia lists on Goodreads to be the most helpful.

PRO TIP: If you use stock photo images for your book cover, buy a commercial license. Print a copy of the license and the order confirmation, and keep these documents on file.

PRO TIP: Most of my covers require composites of multiple stock photos. Track photo costs and include these in your book cover budget. If working with a professional book cover designer, ask if stock photo costs are included in their price quote.

CHAPTER 7: ARCS

ARC stands for Advance Reader Copy or Advance Reading Copy and is a proof copy of your book that can be sent out to reviewers prior to release. ARCs are not for sale and often come with disclaimers on the cover and/or on the copyright page letting the reader know that this copy may vary from the final published book.

The goal of sending out ARCs to reviewers is to gather early reviews and create excitement about your upcoming release. It is important to get ARCs out to reviewers as early as possible, but be wary of sending out an early draft containing multiple errors. Even with a large disclaimer stating that an ARC is an uncorrected proof copy, I've seen scathing reviews targeting grammar or punctuation errors. Try to use a draft that is as close to your final draft as possible for your ARCs.

Formatting is also important. But how do I make my ARCs available in multiple formats before release?

I will show you a few quick and easy formatting tips below. These are tips for getting your ARCs out to reviewers before your book's release. Comprehensive information on how to format your book for ebook and for print can be found in later chapters.

Ebook ARCs:

Ebook ARCs are the easiest, fastest, and cheapest way to make your book available to reviewer's worldwide. There are no printing costs, no shipping costs, and your book can be sent instantly by email or cloud. If you don't want to handle the direct distribution of your ebook ARCs, there are companies you can use to get your eARCs to reviewers.

eARC Distributors:
- NetGalley

- BookFunnel

PRO TIP: NetGalley (www.netgalley.com) is a great way to get eARCs in the hands of reviewers, but, while their pricing for indie authors has come down in recent years, their service is expensive (around $399 to list a title for six months). If you are looking to save money, consider joining a professional organization that offers a reduced group rate for NetGalley. SFWA offers a reduced rate on approved science fiction or fantasy books from active members and Broad Universe offers a reduced rate (around $30 for one month) on approved speculative fiction books by active members. This NetGalley savings alone can offset your membership dues, and you'll avoid the more lengthy NetGalley registration process required for individual authors and small publishers.

Ebook formatting can be done in a variety of ways. If writing your manuscript in Scrivner, you can export your document to all ebook formats. Draft2Digital and Smashwords will do a lot of the formatting for you. Draft2Digital will create all ebook formats without needing to publish the ebooks, and requires less formatting from you than the Smashwords meatgrinder method. With Draft2Digital you will still need to follow the guidelines in **Chapter 1: Build a Template**, and chapters will need to be formatted with a distinct heading style.

For eARCs, you can also manually create a PDF, which can be easily created in Word, and manually create a Mobi/Prc file that can be read on any Kindle device or app. If you want to manually create a Kindle eARC, you will need a program like MobiPocket.

Note: Mobipocket is a quick and easy way to make early copies of your book available for reading on a Kindle device. Long before creating ARCs for reviewers, I create manual Kindle files as part of my editing process.

I've discovered that I will spot different spelling and punctuation errors when reading my first draft in different formats, so I create a Kindle file as part of my self-editing. This helps me to do a first round edit away from my laptop screen and without printing out hundreds of double-spaced pages. My eyes get a break from the computer screen, I can do a round of edits easily while traveling, and I catch errors that I might otherwise miss on a paper printout or computer screen. This leads to a cleaner second draft for my beta readers and a cleaner third draft for my editor, potentially saving me time and money.

HOW TO: Ebook ARC

If using Draft2Digital, Smashwords, or MobiPocket to create your eARC, follow these steps. The initial settings are needed for all of these methods.

To format an eARC, you will need to make changes to some of the settings from the template we began using in **Chapter 1: Build a Writing Template**. **Save** the file under a different name than your manuscript and make the changes listed below.

- Title Page
- Copyright Page
- Chapter Headings
- Page Breaks
- Remove Spaces
- Remove Tabs

Go to the beginning of your document. Go to **Insert**, click **Page Break**, and add a **Title Page**. You will need a centered title and a centered author name. Go to **Insert**, click **Page Break**, and add a **Copyright Page**. You will need a centered title, author name, and copyright year. For your ARC, you can add a disclaimer that this is an uncorrected proof copy.

Set a Heading style for your Chapter Headings. Go to your first chapter or your introduction. **Select/highlight** the chapter name. From the **Home** tab, under **Font,** change the selected chapter heading to **Font Size** 14 pt and **Bold**, under **Paragraph,** click **Center** and change the **First Line** indent to none.

Note: Do not change the Normal style for the entire document. Only change the highlighted chapter heading (Introduction or Chapter 1).

While the chapter heading is still highlighted, move your cursor to **Home**, **Styles**, **Heading 1**, right-click on

Heading 1, and select **Update Heading 1 to Match Selection**. Your Heading 1 style has now been set.

Go to the beginning of each chapter, **select/highlight** the chapter heading, and click **Heading 1**. The heading should change to Font Size 14 pt, Bold, and the First Line indent should be gone, making the chapter heading truly centered. Do this for each chapter heading. **Save** your document.

STOP.

DRAFT2DIGITAL: If uploading to Draft2Digital, you can stop now and upload your Word document. For all other methods, please continue. If you are unsure if you inserted extra spaces or tabs into your document, scroll down for information on how to use Word's advanced **Find and Replace** features to remove these from your document.

CONTINUE.

Page breaks need to be added at the end of each chapter.

PRO TIP: If you are comfortable with multitasking, you can change your chapter headings and insert page breaks at the same time.

From the **Home** tab, click on the **Show/Hide** button that looks like a paragraph symbol. This will reveal all formatting and make it easier to see where you insert your page breaks. Start at the beginning of your document and go to the end of each chapter.

Click your cursor after the final line of your chapter, hit **Enter**, go to the **Insert** tab, and click **Page Break**. Do this for each chapter.

Tabs mess up ebook formatting. Even if you took my advice in Chapter 1, it's a good idea to double-check your work. All it takes is a cat walking over your keyboard and hitting the tab key once to ruin your ebook formatting.

Search for tab spaces in your document. With the Show/Hide button still revealing formatting, go to the beginning of your document. Hold down **CTRL+F** to open the **Find and Replace** window. Click on the **Find** tab. Place your cursor in the **Find What** field. Click the **More** button to reveal more options. Click the **Special** button to find special characters and select **Tab Character**. A carrot symbol and a lowercase "t" will appear in the **Find What** field. Click on the **Find Next** button.

If you get a message that the search symbol was not found, then your document is clean. If there are tabs in your document, remove by deleting the highlighted tab which will appear as an arrow.

Additional spaces at the end of paragraphs can also cause formatting problems for your ebook. We will use Word's Find and Replace feature to remove these extra spaces. With the Show/Hide button still revealing formatting, go to the beginning of your document. Hold down **CTRL+F** to open the **Find and Replace** window. Click on the **Replace** tab. Click the **More** button to reveal more options.

Place your cursor in the **Find What** field and press the **Space Bar** twice. Click the **Special** button for special characters and select **Paragraph Mark**. The **Find What** field should show blank spaces and a paragraph mark. Place your cursor in the **Replace With** field. Click the **Special** button for special characters and select **Paragraph Mark**. The **Find What** field should show a paragraph mark. Click the **Replace All** button.

Repeat using one space to remove one space after paragraphs. Place your cursor in the **Find What** field and press the **Space Bar** once. Click the **Special** button for special characters and select **Paragraph Mark**. The **Find What** field should show a blank space and a paragraph mark. Place your cursor in the **Replace With** field. Click the **Special** button for special characters and select **Paragraph Mark**. The **Find What** field should show a paragraph mark. Click the **Replace All** button. **Save** and **Close** your document.

STOP.

PDF: If you are creating a **PDF**, open your document. Go to **Save As**, put in a new **File Name** such as Title ARC PDF, and select **PDF** as the **Save As Type**. Click the **Save** button. Your PDF ARC is ready to send to send to reviewers.

SMASHWORDS: If you are uploading to **Smashwords**, you will need a **.doc** file. Open your document. Go to **Save As**, put in a new **File Name**, and select **Word 97-2003 Document** as the **Save As Type**. Click the **Save** button. Your **.doc** file is ready to upload to Smashwords, but I don't recommend using this method for ARCs because creating your files with Smashwords will publish your book. If you decide to use this method for an ARC, make sure to remove/unselect all distribution markets in the **Channel Manager** section of your dashboard.

MOBIPOCKET: Note that Mobipocket shut their website down November 2016. If you still have the Mobipocket Creator tool, or if you find a safe site to download the tool from, you can use the directions below.

If creating a Kindle file using **MobiPocket**, you will need an HTML document. Open your document. Go to **Save As**, put in a new **File Name**, and select **Web Page, Filtered** as the **Save As Type**. Click the **Save** button. If prompted with a warning about removing office tags, click **Yes**. Close your document. If you don't have the Mobipocket tool, it's free from the Mobipocket website (www.mobipocket.com). Open **Mobipocket Creator**. Select **Import HTML Document**. Select your HTML file and click the **Import** button. Select your file, select the **Build** icon, and click the **Build** button. Click the **Okay** button. You now have an eARC compatible with Kindle devices and the Kindle for PC reading app.

PRO TIP: If using Smashwords or Draft2Digital to create eARCs, you can download your book in all file types, including ePub, Kindle/Mobi, and PDF.

PRO TIP: **Print** formatting requires **Section Breaks** between chapters. **Next Page** section breaks are used in front and back matter and **Odd Page** section breaks are used in the body of your document. This is different from ebook formatting. **Ebook** formatting requires **Page Breaks** between each chapter and between each page of the front matter and back matter of the book. Using the wrong kind of break in your document will mess up your book's formatting, and break errors can't be fixed using Word's find and replace feature.

Trade Paperback ARCs:
Some reviewers will only accept physical books for review. Thankfully, the ratio of reviewers requiring physical

books has changed in the seven years since I began publishing books. In 2009, more than 75% of reviewers would only accept physical books for review. Now most reviewers prefer ebooks. Ebook ARCs are the fastest and cheapest way to make your book available for review, but sometimes you will need to send out a physical book.

If a reviewer will only accept a physical copy, you can send them a proof copy from Createspace. Even if you decide to use a private print company or a different print-on-demand company like LuLu or IngramSpark for your final print editions, Createspace is the most cost effective way to print advance copies.

HOW TO: Trade Paperback ARC

Read the PRO TIP information below before deciding if ARC formatting will best suit your publishing needs. To format a trade paperback ARC, you will need to make changes to some of the settings from the template we began using in **Chapter 1: Build a Writing Template**. **Save** the file under a different name than your manuscript and make the changes listed below.

- Trim Size
- Different Odd and Even
- Margins 0.6
- Gutter 0.3, Left
- Mirror Margins
- Font Century Schoolbook
- Font Size 11 pt
- Line Spacing Exactly 13.2 pt
- Widow/Orphan Control
- Add Title Page
- Add Copyright Page

In the case of a 6 x 9 trade paperback, go to **Page Layout** and change the **Size** to 6 x 9. On **Page Layout** go to **Margins**, **Custom Margins**, **Layout** and select **Different Odd and Even**. Go to the **Margin** tab and set all **Margins** to 0.6. Set **Gutter** to 0.3 and **Gutter Position** to Left. Under **Multiple Pages** select **Mirror Margins**.

Go to **Home**, **Styles**, and click the small **Arrow** at the bottom right of the **Styles** section. Click on **Normal** and select

Modify from the drop down arrow to the right. Click the **Format** button and select **Font**. Change the **Font Size** to 11 pt.

Click the **Format** button and select **Paragraph** and set the **Line Spacing** to Exactly 13.2 pt. Under the **Line and Page Breaks** tab make sure that **Widow and Orphan Control** is checked off.

Insert a title page and copyright page at the beginning of your document. Since this is an ARC, fancy fonts do not need to be used. Go to **Page Layout, Breaks, Section Break**, and select **Next Page** to insert a title page and type in your book's title centered and your name centered. Go to **Page Layout, Breaks, Section Break**, and select **Odd Page** to insert the copyright page. The copyright page should include your book's title, copyright year, ISBN, and any disclaimers. For your ARC you can add a disclaimer that this is an uncorrected proof copy.

To keep our ARC simple, we are not doing fancy formatting at the beginning of each chapter or adding in headers with the page numbers and alternating book title and author name. Information on setting a Heading style for chapter headings and adding headers can be found in **Chapter 9: Print Formatting**.

We do need to add a section break between each chapter. From the **Home** tab click on the **Show/Hide** button that looks like a paragraph symbol. This will reveal all formatting and make it easier to see where you insert your section breaks. Start at the beginning of your document and go to end of each chapter.

Click your cursor after the final line of your chapter, hit **Enter**, go to the **Page Layout** tab, **Breaks, Section Break**, and select **Odd Page**. Do this for each chapter.

Save your document as a PDF. In Word, this is done by going to the **Start** button, **Save As**, and selecting **PDF**. Do not click save. We need to embed all fonts, especially if you decided to add any special custom font styles on your title page. Check the **Optimize for Standard** option. Click the drop down arrow for **Tools** located beside the Save button. Select **Save Options** and check **Embed All Fonts in this File**. Uncheck

Do Not Embed System Fonts. Click **Okay** and click the **Save** button. Close the document.

Verify that all fonts are embedded. Open the **PDF** copy of your document. Go to **File**, **Properties**, and click on the **Fonts** tab. Check to make sure that each font has **Embedded Subset** listed beside the font name. If it does not, then the font is not embedded in your PDF.

In addition to the print book's interior file, you will need to upload a wrap-around cover. For an ARC, this does not have to feature the final cover art. During my years as a book reviewer, I rarely received ARCs with final cover art. You can design your cover to be a simple white cover with black text.

For a 6 x 9 trade paperback, the overall width of your book cover is 12.25 inches plus the spine width. Spine width for a book with white pages printed through Createspace is 0.002252 x number of pages. Check the number of pages in your PDF. The height of your book is 9.25 inches. Set a margin of 0.125 from the outside edges and do not place text outside these margins. If adding text to your ARC's spine, allow for a variance of 0.0625.

Save your book cover as a **PDF**.

If you are new to **Createspace** (www.createspace.com), set up an account. Go to your **Member Dashboard** and click on the blue **Add New Title** button beside **My Projects**. Fill in the book and author information. Make sure that the ISBN is correct before proceeding.

Upload book interior PDF and book cover PDF. Your files will be considered for review. When your files pass the approval process, you can order proof copies. Do **not** approve proof for release. When ordering proof copies for ARCs, you will need to change the quantity from the default of one copy to the number of copies you need to send to reviewers.

PRO TIP: The tutorial for creating a Trade Paperback ARC above does not include all book formatting for the book's interior or exterior. This makes the ARC faster and easier to produce, and allows for getting an ARC cover created before your final cover has been received from your cover artist. But there are no rules against using a final copy as an ARC.

If your book has been through its final round of professional edits, you have your final cover art, and you either have the time to complete all formatting (details in **Chapter 9: Print Formatting**) or you've received your formatted files from a professional, you can upload all of your final files now. You can use your final proof copies as ARCs easily by including a cover letter with each copy stating that this is an ARC for review. Just make sure not to approve your book for sale. All books ordered as proof copies prior to release will also have PROOF printed in large, bold letters in the back of the book.

CHAPTER 8: EBOOK FORMATTING

The largest percentage of indie book sales comes from ebooks. In fact, self-published authors are now beating out the Big 5 traditional publishers with ebook sales on Amazon and represent a very healthy third of author sales on the other ebook retailers.

In the US, more than 90% of ebook sales go through four retailers. Amazon leads the pack with over 70% of the ebook market. Apple's iBooks comes in a distant second with about 10% of ebook sales. Barnes & Noble and Kobo make up about 3-6% each.

In this chapter, you'll learn how to format your book for these major ebook retailers. In the HOW TO section, I'll provide a detailed tutorial on ebook formatting, and an extended tutorial gives instructions on how to publish direct through Amazon KDP.

There are two distributors that, for a royalty percentage, will handle some of the final steps of your ebook formatting and distribute your ebook to your choice of retailers. In the case of Smashwords, you can also sell your ebooks to libraries. What Smashwords and Draft2Digital can't do (yet) is distribute your ebook to Amazon. Even if you use one of these services to distribute your ebooks to all other retailers, you will need to learn your way around the Amazon KDP dashboard.

I'll also try to save you from the most common ebook formatting mistakes. Even if you decide to hire a professional to format your book, knowing the pitfalls of ebook formatting will help save you time and money.

Formatting:
Ebook formatting can be done in a variety of ways. If writing your manuscript in Scrivner, you can export your document to all ebook formats. Draft2Digital and Smashwords

will do a lot of the formatting for you. Draft2Digital will create all ebook formats for you without needing to publish the ebooks, and requires less formatting from you than the Smashwords meatgrinder method. With Draft2Digital, you will still need to follow the guidelines in **Chapter 1: Build a Template** and your book's chapters will need to be formatted with a distinct Heading style as explained in detail below.

HOW TO: Ebook Formatting

To format an ebook, you will need to make changes to some of the settings from the template we began using in **Chapter 1: Build a Writing Template. Save** the file under a different name than your manuscript and make the changes listed below.

- Title Page
- Copyright Page
- Author Page
- Chapter Headings
- Page Breaks
- Remove Spaces
- Remove Tabs
- Save in Correct Format

Insert your book's front matter. Go to the beginning of your document. Go to **Insert**, click **Page Break**, and add a **Title Page**. You will need a centered title and a centered author name. Go to **Insert**, click **Page Break**, and add a **Copyright Page**. You will need a centered title, author name, and copyright year.

Insert your book's back matter. Go to the end of your document. Go to **Insert**, click **Page Break**, and add an **Author Page**. You will need a short author bio. A professional author photo is recommended, but not required. If you include an author photo, do not copy and paste a photo into your ebook. Go to the **Insert** tab, **Picture**, and select your author photo.

Set a Heading style for your Chapter Headings. Go to your first chapter or your introduction. **Select/highlight** the chapter name. From the **Home** tab, under the **Font** section, change the selected chapter heading to **Font Size** 14 pt and

Bold, under **Paragraph** click **Center** and change the **First Line** indent to none.

Note: Do not change the Normal style for the entire document. Only change the highlighted chapter heading (Introduction or Chapter 1).

While the chapter heading is still highlighted, move your cursor to **Home**, **Styles**, **Heading 1**, right-click on **Heading 1**, and select **Update Heading 1 to Match Selection**. Your Heading 1 style has now been set.

Go to the beginning of each chapter, **select/highligh**t the chapter heading, and click **Heading 1**. The heading should change to Font Size 14 pt, Bold, and the First Line indent should be gone, making the chapter heading truly centered. Do this for each chapter heading. **Save** your document.

STOP.

DRAFT2DIGITAL: If uploading to Draft2Digital, you can stop now and upload your Word document. For all other methods, please continue. If you are unsure if you inserted extra spaces or tabs into your document, scroll down for information on how to use Word's advanced find and replace feature to remove from your document.

CONTINUE.

Page breaks need to be added at the end of each chapter.

PRO TIP: If you are comfortable with multitasking, you can change your chapter headings and insert page breaks at the same time.

NOTE: If uploading direct to Nook Press and using a Word file ONLY, section breaks will need to be used in place of page breaks. This is the one exception in all ebook retailer upload methods. **All other ebook formatting requires page breaks.**

From the **Home** tab click on the **Show/Hide** button that looks like a paragraph symbol. This will reveal all formatting and make it easier to see where you insert your page breaks. Start at the beginning of your document and go to the end of each chapter.

Click your cursor after the final line of your chapter, hit **Enter**, go to the **Insert** tab, and click **Page Break**. Do this for each chapter.

Search for tab spaces in your document. With the **Show/Hide** button still revealing formatting, go to the beginning of your document. Hold down **CTRL+F** to open the **Find and Replace** window. Click on the **Find** tab. Place your cursor in the **Find What** field. Click the **More** button to reveal more options. Click the **Special** button to find special characters and select **Tab Character**. A carrot symbol and a lowercase "t" will appear in the **Find What** field. Click on the **Find Next** button. If you get a message that the search symbol was not found, then your document is clean. If there are tabs in your document, remove by deleting the highlighted tab which will appear as an arrow.

Additional spaces at the end of paragraphs can also cause formatting problems for your ebook. We will use Word's Find and Replace feature to remove these extra spaces. With the Show/Hide button still revealing formatting, go to the beginning of your document. Hold down **CTRL+F** to open the **Find and Replace** window. Click on the **Replace** tab. Click the **More** button to reveal more options. Place your cursor in the **Find What** field and press the **Space Bar** twice. Click the **Special** button for special characters and select **Paragraph Mark**. The **Find What** field should show blank spaces and a paragraph mark. Place your cursor in the **Replace With** field. Click the **Special** button for special characters and select **Paragraph Mark**. The **Find What** field should show a paragraph mark. Click the **Replace All** button.

Repeat using one space to remove one space after paragraphs. Place your cursor in the **Find What** field and press the **Space Bar** once. Click the **Special** button for special characters and select **Paragraph Mark**. The **Find What** field should show a blank space and a paragraph mark. Place your cursor in the **Replace With** field. Click the **Special** button for special characters and select **Paragraph Mark**. The **Find What** field should show a paragraph mark. Click the **Replace All** button. **Save** and **Close** your document.

STOP.

SMASHWORDS: If you are uploading to **Smashwords**, you will need a **.doc** file. Open your document. Go to **Save As**, put in a new **File Name**, and select **Word 97-2003 Document** as the **Save As Type**. Click the **Save** button. Your **.doc** file is ready to upload to Smashwords.

NOOK PRESS: If you are uploading direct to Barnes & Noble's Nook Press (formerly PubIt!), you will need a Word .doc or .docx file, ePub, or HTML. At this time, Nook Press does not support uploads of ZIP files, so HTML files cannot include images. In my experience, uploading direct to Nook Press is the most troublesome. They are also the only distributor that, when uploading a Word file, require section breaks instead of page breaks between chapters. If that is the method you choose, make a note of the change when following the instructions below. If you don't have advanced skills with formatting an ePub file I highly recommend using Scrivener, Smashwords, or Draft2Digital to create your file for you.

CONTINUE.

You will need to manually add a Table of Contents (TOC) to your document to make it ready for Amazon KDP.

Insert your **Table of Contents** near the beginning of your book. After your front matter (title page, copyright page), left click your cursor and go to **Insert** and click the **Page Break** button. You will now have a new blank page. At the top of the blank page, type **Table of Contents** and hit **Enter**. Go to the **References** tab, click the **Table of Contents** button, and select **Insert Table of Contents**. From the new **Table of Contents** window, uncheck **Show Page Numbers**, and for **Show Levels,** select 1. Click the **Okay** button.

Your Table of Contents should appear. Now **highlight/select** the words **Table of Contents**. Go to the **Insert** tab, from the **Links** section click on **Bookmarks**. In the **Bookmark Name** field, type in **toc**. Click the **Add** button.

If you receive a last minute edit or make a later revision, remember to update your Table of Contents. Click your cursor anywhere in the TOC and hit the **F9 key** on your keyboard. Your TOC should now be updated.

Save and close your document.

You need to convert your document to HTML. Open your document. Go to **Save As**, put in a new **File Name**, and select **Web Page, Filtered** as the **Save As Type**. Click the

Save button. If prompted with a warning about removing office tags, click **Yes**. Close your document.

NO PHOTOS: If you have no images in your book, not even an author photo at the back of the book, then you are done and ready to upload your book's HTML document to Amazon KDP.

PHOTOS: If you have images in your book, you need to create a compressed ZIP file. Go to the folder where you saved your book's HTML file. You'll see a **Folder** with your images and an **HTML** file. **Right-click** on the **HTML** file, move your cursor to **Send To**, and select **Compressed (Zipped) Folder**. A **ZIP Folder** will appear with a zipper on it. **Drag** the original **folder** with your images in it onto the **ZIP Folder**.

UPLOADING TO AMAZON KDP: You will need to create an **Amazon KDP** (kdp.amazon.com) account. Don't forget to provide your payment information in the **Account** section so that you receive your royalties.

To publish your book, go to the **Bookshelf** tab on your dashboard, and click on the **Create New Title** button. Only check off the Enroll in KDP Select box if you are willing to publish exclusively to Amazon.

Fill out your book's details, including **Book Name** (title), **Publisher** (name you are publishing under and bought your ISBNs as), **Description** (blurb/description). Under **Book Contributors**, click the **Add Contributors** button, put in your author name, and select **Author**. Verify your publishing rights by selecting that your book is not public domain. Add **Categories** and **Keywords** to help readers find your book on Amazon (more on categories and keywords in **Chapter 10: SEO, Keywords, and BISAC Categories**). Select your book release option by checking off if you want to publish your book now or if you are setting this book up for a pre-order. Upload your **Book Cover** by clicking the **Browse for Image** button, and select your high resolution cover image.

Upload your book file by going to **Book Content File**, clicking the **Browse** button, and selecting your book's interior file. If your book does not have images, select the HTML file. If your book has images, select the ZIP Folder.

Once your interior file is uploaded and converted you can use the **Preview** feature to make sure that your book's interior looks correct on all Kindle devices.

Click the **Save and Continue** button. Enter your **Pricing** information. When you are done, agree to Amazon's terms, and click **Save**.

Note: More on your Amazon dashboard and book page in **Chapter 11: Retail Product Pages**.

PRO TIP: Keep your ebook formatting simple. Every added symbol, image, and space increases the chances of a poor reader experience.

CHAPTER 9: PRINT BOOK FORMATTING

Print books are a much smaller part of the market for indie authors, but print sales are on the rise. With the ease of using free or low cost print on demand (POD) companies like Createspace (www.createspace.com), LuLu (www.lulu.com), and IngramSpark (www.ingramcontent.com), authors are able to create and distribute print editions of their books worldwide.

Using the tutorial in the HOW TO section below, I'll show you basic print book formatting and guide you through the process of uploading your book through Createspace.

Createspace is an Amazon owned company and is the best way to get your print books on Amazon. It is also a great way to get your print books sold through online retailers.

You can use Createspace to distribute worldwide, but you do not have to. Many brick-and-mortar book stores will not carry books printed by an Amazon owned company. Books distributed through IngramSpark have a better chance of being sold in brick-and-mortar stores when you select the larger wholesaler discount and accept returns.

While there is a chance of selling more print books with this method, there are also more risks for the self-publisher. IngramSpark does not offer the free ISBN option (see **Chapter 4: ISBNs and Barcodes** for my recommendations on how to get your own ISBNs), so if you were planning on using a free ISBN and letting Createspace be listed as your book's publisher, you already have an additional expense. IngramSpark also has a setup fee and an annual market access fee, sometimes referred to a market distribution fee. In order to entice retailers, you will also have to accept a smaller royalty, accept returns (a hard to predict expense that can send an indie author into the red), and direct some of your promotions at brick-and-mortar retailers.

With enough legwork, professional press releases and sell sheets (more info in the Super Simple Quick Start Guide to Book Marketing), and a willingness to do in-store readings and book signings, there is the potential for more book sales by selling through brick-and-mortar stores, but weigh the risks. If you decide to only sell to Amazon through Createspace, select only Amazon and Amazon Europe under sales channels. Do not select any of the options under expanded distribution. Then use IngramSpark to distribute to all other sales channels. If you do not want to pay for IngramSpark, select bookstores and online retailers under expanded distribution. Note that Createspace used to charge for expanded distribution, but that service is now free.

Whether you use one of the Print-On-Demand companies above, or use a private print company to print your books, the tutorial below with give you helpful, basic tips for print book formatting. Since Createspace is the most popular way to self-publish a print book, the tutorial is optimized for uploading to Createspace. Always check the style guide for your print company before formatting your book.

Keep in mind that the formatting recommended here is intended for publishing a professional quality book with basic formatting skills. If you want more advanced features, you will need to continue beyond this tutorial or hire a professional, like Polgarus Studio (www.polgarusstudio.com), to handle your print book's interior formatting.

You can also customize your book somewhat by varying from the tutorial when it comes to your document's font styles. Just use caution and save your document under a different file name. The font style for the body of your book can be changed, but you will need to find the best font size and line spacing for any alternate font style. Font style and font size can be nearly anything you want for your chapter headings so long as you are consistent with your heading style and you embed all fonts when converting your file to PDF.

HOW TO: To format a print book, you will need to make changes to some of the settings from the template we began using in **Chapter 1: Build a Writing Template. Save** the

file under a different name than your manuscript and make the changes listed below.
- Trim Size
- Different Odd and Even
- Margins 0.6
- Gutter 0.3, Left
- Mirror Margins
- Font Century Schoolbook
- Font Size 11 pt
- Line Spacing Exactly 13.2 pt
- Widow/Orphan Control
- Add Front Matter
- Add Back Matter
- Headers and Page Numbers

Your document page size will need to match your book's **trim size**. In the case of a 6 x 9 trade paperback, the most popular print book size for indie authors, go to **Page Layout** and in the **Page Setup** section, click the **Size** button. Select **More Paper Sizes** and in the **Paper** tab change the **Size** to 6 x 9 and click **OK**.

On **Page Layout** go to **Margins**, **Custom Margins**, **Layout** and select **Different Odd and Even**. Go to the **Margin** tab and set all **Margins** to 0.6. Set **Gutter** to 0.3 and **Gutter Position** to Left. Under **Multiple Pages** select **Mirror Margins**.

Go to **Home**, **Styles**, and click the small **Arrow** at the bottom right below the Change Styles button. Click on **Normal** and select **Modify** from the drop down arrow to the right. Click the **Format** button and select **Font**. Change the **Font Size** to 11 pt.

Click the **Format** button and select **Paragraph** and the **Line Spacing** to Exactly 13.2 pt. Under the **Line and Page Breaks** tab make sure that **Widow and Orphan Control** is checked.

We need to add your book's front matter by inserting a title page and copyright page at the beginning of your document.

TITLE PAGE: Go to **Page Layout**, **Breaks**, **Section Break**, and select **Next Page** to insert a title page and type in your book's title centered and your name centered.

Highlight/select the text on your title page, from the **Home** tab go to **Paragraph** and click the Center button. Click the **Line Spacing** button and under **Indentation** change the **Special** spacing from First Line indent to **None**. Now the text on your title page is centered.

You can use a custom font on your title page to match the title font on your book cover. A tutorial on how to load a custom font is in the HOW TO section of **Chapter 5: Font Licensing**. If you use a custom font, or want to increase the font size of the font on your title page, **highlight/select** your title. Remember, we are only changing the font style, font size, and line spacing for the highlighted selections. Do not change these settings for the entire document.

From the **Home** tab, go to **Font** and change the **Font Style** and/or **Font Size**. You may notice that some of your text has disappeared. No worries! With your title still highlighted, from to the **Home** tab go to **Paragraph** and click the **Line Spacing** button. Change **Line Spacing** to **Single**. Now the text on your title page should show on your screen. Follow the same steps if you'd like to change the font style or font size for the author name text on your title page.

COPYRIGHT PAGE: Go to **Page Layout**, **Breaks**, **Section Break**, and select **Odd Page** to insert the copyright page. The copyright page should include your book's title, copyright year, ISBN, publisher, author name, and any disclaimers.

Look inside books within your genre to see how those copyright pages are typically set up. I recommend a page with left alignment and no first line indent. **Highlight/select** the text on your copyright page. From the **Home** tab go the **Paragraph** section and click the **Left Alignment** button, then click the **Line Spacing** button and under **Indentation** change **Special** to **None**.

BACK MATTER: Insert your book's back matter. Go to the end of your document. Go to **Page Layout**, click **Section Break** and select **Odd Page**, and add an **Author Page**. You will need a short author bio. A professional author photo is recommended but not required. If you include an author photo, do not copy and paste a photo into your book. Go to the **Insert** tab, **Picture**, and select your author photo. If you add a link to your website and your word processing program changes your URL to an active link, remove the link by **right-clicking** on the link and selecting **Remove Hyperlink**. This will keep your website link text from looking faded on the printed page.

CHAPTER HEADINGS: Set a heading style for your chapter headings. You can use nearly any font style and font size for your chapter headings. For the sake of this tutorial, I have selected a basic system font. Go to your first chapter, which, depending on the book, will be Chapter 1 or your Introduction. **Select/highlight** the chapter name. From the **Home** tab, under the **Font** section change the selected chapter heading to **Font Style** Courier, **Font Size** 14 pt and **Bold**. Under **Paragraph** click the **Center** button, then click the **Line Spacing** button, go under **Indentation** and change the **Special** first line indent to none. Note: Do not change the Normal style for the entire document. Only change the highlighted chapter heading.

While the chapter heading is still highlighted, move your cursor to **Home**, **Styles**, **Heading 1**, right-click on **Heading 1**, and select **Update Heading 1 to Match Selection**. Your Heading 1 style has now been set.

Go to the beginning of each chapter, **select/highlight** the chapter heading, and click **Heading 1**. The heading should change to the Font Style Courier, Font Size 14 pt, Bold, and the First Line indent should be gone, making the chapter heading truly centered. Do this for each chapter heading in your document.

DROP CAPS: Some books boldface or use drop caps for the first letter of the first paragraph for each chapter. **Highlight/select** the first letter from the first paragraph at the beginning of your first chapter. If you just want to make the first letter bold, then go to the **Home** tab, the **Font** section, and click the **Bold** button. If you want to add drop caps, go to the **Insert** tab, the **Text** section, and click the **Drop Cap** button. From the drop down menu select **Dropped**. If you want to customize the **Font Style** or the number of **Lines to Drop**, select **Drop Cap Options** to change the default. If you use a custom font for your drop caps, make sure you have the rights to use that font for commercial use (see **Chapter 5: Font Licensing**) and embed the font when saving your document to PDF (see below).

SECTION BREAKS: We need to add a section break between each chapter. From the **Home** tab click on the **Show/Hide** button that looks like a paragraph symbol. This will reveal all formatting and make it easier to see where you insert your section breaks. Start at the beginning of your document and go to end of each chapter.

Click your cursor after the final line of your chapter, hit **Enter**, go to the **Page Layout** tab, **Breaks**, **Section Break**, and select **Odd Page**. Do this for each chapter.

HEADERS AND PAGE NUMBERS: Headers, also known as Running Heads, are added after section breaks have been inserted. Look at interior book design for print books in your genre. Standard practice for most books is to have no headers or page numbers in the front matter or back matter, and no headers or page numbers on the first page of each chapter in the body of your book. The most common book design is to have page numbers in the header, positioned at the page's outer edge and aligned with the chapter's text, and to have the author name in the header on even pages and the title displayed in all capital letters in the header on odd pages. The author name and book title positioning is either centered or about 10 spaces from the page number. For the sake of this tutorial, we'll use this standard for the header and page numbering design.

Note: Creating Running Heads is the most error prone part of print book formatting. Before attempting this step it is advisable to **save** your document under a new name. If things go terribly wrong, you'll have a clean draft to go back to.

Go to your first chapter and **double-click** on the empty space at the top of the page to open the **Header/Footer** menu. If you have any trouble opening the menu, go to the **Insert** tab and click the **Header** button. From the **Header** button click **Edit Header**, and make sure that the **Different First Page** and **Different Odd and Even** boxes are checked.

You will see that it says two things along the dotted line marking the header. The section number is given and whether or not the section is connected to the previous section. The default is **Same as Previous**. When the feature is on it will be highlighted in orange. We do not want our headers for our chapters to be connected to the front matter of the book. Go to the **Navigation** section of the **Header/Footer** toolbar and click **Link to Previous**, turning this feature **OFF**.

Now it's time to set up your running heads.

With your cursor in the **Even Page Header** for chapter 1, click the **Page Number** button, select **Top of Page** and **Simple Plain Number 1**. Your page number will appear aligned left, but it will be indented. We need to remove the indent. **Highlight/select** the **Page Number** and go to the **Home** tab **Paragraph** section, click the **Line Spacing** button and under **Indentation** change **Special** to none. The page number should now appear at the left edge of your header. Click the cursor to the right of the page number, press the **Space Bar** 10 times (see what looks best and adjust), and type the **Author Name**.

Now still in chapter 1, the same numbered section, follow the same steps to open a header on an odd page. If the odd header says that it is **Same as Previous**, click the **Link to Previous** button to turn this feature **OFF**. Future chapters will be linked, but not the body of the book with the front matter.

With your cursor in the **Odd Page Header**, click the **Page Number** button, select **Top of Page** and **Simple Plain Number 3**. Your page number will appear aligned left, but it will be indented. We need to remove the indent. **Highlight/select** the **Page Number** and go to the **Home** tab **Paragraph** section, click the **Line Spacing** button and under **Indentation** change **Special** to none. The page number should now appear at the right edge of your header. Click the cursor to the left of the page number, press the **Space Bar** 10 times (see what looks best and adjust), and type the **Book Title**. If you want, you can use the same font as your title on the title page, but press **Caps Lock** and type your title in all capital letters.

Scroll through your document and make sure you like the design for your running headers. Check that there are no running headers in your book's Front Matter. Also, go to the end of your book and unselect **Same as Previous** in your Author Bio so that no running headers display in your end matter.

SAVE AS PDF: Save your document as a PDF. In Word, this is done by going to the **Start** button, **Save As**, and selecting **PDF**. Do not click save yet. We need to embed all fonts, especially if you decided to add any special custom font styles for your chapter headings, running header, or on your title page. Check the **Optimize for Standard** option. Click the drop down arrow for **Tools** located beside the **Save** button. Select **Save Options** and check **Embed All Fonts in this File**. Uncheck **Do Not Embed System Fonts**. Click **Okay** and click the **Save** button. Close the document.

Verify that all fonts are embedded. Open the **PDF** copy of your document. Go to **File**, **Properties**, and click on the **Fonts** tab. Check to make sure that each font has **Embedded Subset** listed beside the font name. If not, the font is not embedded in your PDF.

In addition to the print book's interior file, you will need to upload a wrap-around cover.

For a 6 x 9 trade paperback, the overall width of your book cover is 12.25 inches plus the spine width. Spine width for a book with white pages printed through Createspace is 0.002252 x number of pages. Check the number of pages in your PDF. The height of your book is 9.25 inches. Set a margin of 0.125 from the outside edges and do not place text outside these margins. When adding text to your book's spine, allow for a variance of 0.0625.

Save your book cover as a **PDF**.

CREATESPACE: If you are new to Createspace (www.createspace.com), set up an account. Go to your **Member Dashboard** and click on the blue **Add New Title** button beside **My Projects**. Fill in the book and author information. Make sure that the ISBN is correct before proceeding.

Upload book interior PDF and book cover PDF. Your files will be considered for review. When your files pass the approval process, you can order proof copies. You can use the online proofing tool, but this will only show you the book's interior. I highly recommend ordering a physical proof copy of your book to check for both interior and exterior errors. When you have checked your book and are confident that there are no errors, approve the proof copy.

Now you are ready to sell your book! Go to the **Distribute** tab for your book and click on **Channels**. If you have not already, go to **Standard Distribution** and approve your book for sale on **Amazon.com** and **Amazon Europe**. If you are using IngramSpark for expanded distribution, you are done. If you are using Createspace for all print distribution, scroll down to **Expanded Distribution** and select **Bookstores and Online Retailers**.

CHAPTER 10:
SEO, KEYWORDS, AND BISAC

Understanding SEO, keywords, and BISAC subject codes is essential to aiding your book's discoverability. If you do a quick online search, you'll see that there are millions of published books competing for reader attention. As a fantasy author, for example, you'll be pitting your book against over 1.2 million fantasy books on Amazon alone. This chapter will help you learn what words are important to your book's success and where to use them.

SEO: Search Engine Optimization (SEO) is the process of increasing online visibility. The basic goal of SEO is to drive traffic and improve rankings by pushing your site and content to the top of search engine results. As an author, you want people to be able to find you and your books.

Once you learn SEO, it can be applied to multiple aspects of your book such as title, series name, cover blurb, and product page. SEO can also help improve the visibility of your blog posts, social networking posts, and author bio.

The good news for writers is that the most important SEO tool we have is words. Using the right words makes sites more search engine friendly and can move your book to the top of retailer search results. See the section below on finding the best keywords for you and your books.

Another important tool of SEO is back-links. Back-links are when a webpage other than your own links back to your website. The more back-links to your site (author website, blog, book product page), the higher search engines will rank your site. If you want your site to appear at the top of search results, you need to encourage back-links.

Back-links often occur when a blogger reviews your book or posts an interview or guest post to their blog and social media sites. Providing ARCs to reviewers (more info in

Chapter 7: ARCs), participating in interviews, and writing guest posts are important, but do not forget to provide bloggers and other members of the press with links to your sites. Include your site links on business cards, promotional materials, sell sheets, email signature, press releases, online media kit, and in all direct correspondence with the press. Make it easy for bloggers and other members of the press to add back-links to their articles, reviews, interviews, and guest posts.

PRO TIP: Do not try to game the system. Many companies will try to sell back-links to your site with the claim that it will improve your site's search results, but search engines like Google are skilled at finding and punishing sites that try to cheat their search algorithms. At best, you will have wasted money. At worst, your site may be blacklisted by Google, Bing, or Yahoo. Rely on your site's content and strategic use of keywords rather than paid shortcuts.

KEYWORDS: Keywords are words or short phrases that describe you, your website, or your book. These are the words that readers will use as search terms when performing a search on a search engine like Google, Bing, or Yahoo, or on a retailer like Amazon. For the purposes of this guide, we'll focus on keywords for your book.

Keywords must be relevant and accurately portray your book's content. If a search engine discovers you are trying to cheat the system and load in irrelevant keywords, they can and will blacklist you. Create a list of terms or phrases that describe your book. Consider your book's setting, character, plot, theme, and tone.

What categories does your book fit into? Add categories and subcategories to your list. These do not need to follow BISAC categories. Think about categories where your book might be shelved in a library or bookstore (romance) and categories or labels that book reviewers might use (paranormal romance, regency romance, contemporary romance) when describing your book.

To find the best keywords for your book, perform a search for books in your genre. Think like a customer. If you wanted to buy a book like yours, what words would you use in an online search? Make a list of the search words that you use. What words are relevant to your book, but have less competition? If there is less competition, your book will appear higher in search results.

When selecting keywords, you will need to find a balance between quantity and quality. You want to increase visibility to stimulate a large quantity of visits, but you also want those visitors to be quality visitors who will be interested in your books. General keywords like fiction or mystery will reach more people. Specific keywords and phrases like female sleuth or spy thriller will target a smaller group of readers.

Some authors already have a built in fan base. Knowing the words that your fans are using to find you can help in creating keywords for your next book. If you have a blog or website, look at what keywords most frequently bring readers to your site. Do the words that drive traffic to your website also apply to your book?

Once you have a preliminary list of keywords, you'll need to test the words on Google Adwords and on Amazon. There are two types of keywords: SEO keywords that will increase traffic from sources outside an online retailer and the keywords that will perform best when a reader is searching within a retailer website.

Google Adwords is the best place to test your SEO keywords. Keyword Planner is a free Google Adwords tool designed to provide statistics and determine how keywords will perform. You will need a Google Adwords account to use the Keyword Planner (adwords.google.com/keywordplanner) tool. Keyword Planner can be used to research keywords and get historical statistics and traffic forecasts. In addition to the free keyword tool, you can run an inexpensive ad with Google Adwords to test your keywords.

Amazon is the best place to test retailer keywords. Go to Amazon and begin a search using your keywords. When entering words into a search, Amazon's auto-complete will suggest keywords. It is important to pay attention to what keywords and phrases Amazon suggests. The top suggestions are the power performers. Note that long-tail keywords currently perform better in Amazon searches than short-tail keywords. These are unwieldy for including in book titles, but long-tail keywords are effective when used as the seven keywords for your product page. We'll discuss short-tail versus long-tail keywords in the HOW TO section below.

Now that you've narrowed down your keywords, begin working your keywords into your title, series name, book description, and author bio. Each retailer will also allow a certain number of keywords to be entered in a keywords field in your book's dashboard. These keywords will become part of your book's product page.

Some retailers, like Amazon, have strict rules about the keywords that may be added in your book's product page from your author dashboard. In the case of Amazon, you are allowed seven words or short phrases and they must adhere to Amazon's keyword policy. Learn more about choosing Amazon keywords in this chapter's HOW TO section. This is crucial to creating your book's Amazon product page which we'll discuss next in **Chapter 11: Retail Product Pages**.

PRO TIP: Amazon allows seven keywords. A common misconception is that this means a book can only have seven words in the keyword section. This is false. Amazon now allows long-tail keywords. Phrases using multiple words are acceptable and count as one keyword.

BISAC: BISAC is an acronym for Book Industry Standards and Communications. The BISAC Subject Headings List, also known as the BISAC Subject Code List, is the industry standard list for subject headings and their nine-character alphanumeric code. These headings and corresponding codes tell people in the book trade the primary and secondary store sections where a book will fit best and sell best, helping with database searching and acting as shelving guides.

Knowing the book industry's headings and codes will help you market your book directly to libraries and retailers and will get your book shelved more quickly. Amazon KDP uses BISAC codes. You will need to select your book's primary and secondary BISAC codes when setting up your book through Amazon KDP. Making the best BISAC code selections will ensure your book is properly categorized, increasing your book's visibility with the right readers and improving customer satisfaction.

The BISAC Subject Headings List has fifty major sections. The list is available free at BISG online (bisg.org/page/BISACsubjectcodes). The first step is to choose the major heading which best describes your book. Click on the major heading to see more specific headings in that category.

EXAMPLE: Let's pretend that your book is a post-apocalyptic novel for young adults. Clicking on the major category Young Adult Fiction will reveal a description of the category and a list of specific categories within Young Adult Fiction. "YAF003000 YOUNG ADULT FICTION / Apocalyptic & Post-Apocalyptic" looks like a good fit for your book. YAF003000 is the BISAC alphanumeric code, YOUNG ADULT FICTION is the major category, and Apocalyptic & Post-Apocalyptic is the more specific categorization which will help libraries and book retailers know where to shelve your book and will help readers discover and purchase your book.

Amazon allows for two BISAC categories. Do not be redundant. If you have already selected Young Adult Fiction > Apocalyptic & Post-Apocalyptic, then do not also select Young Adult Fiction. There are many additional categories to choose from, and providing a second specific category will help your book's visibility.

Some categories have keyword prerequisites on Amazon and Amazon.UK. Additional information on how to access Amazon's special category keyword requirements in the HOW TO section below.

PRO TIP: Include your book's BISAC subject codes on sell sheets. Unlike your Amazon product page, you are not limited to just two codes. On your sell sheets, include all of the BISAC codes that you think best fit your book. Sell sheets are an important tool in marketing your book to libraries and booksellers. You can learn more about sell sheets in the **Super Simple Quick Start Guide to Book Marketing**.

HOW TO: Amazon has a keyword policy that restricts what words and phrases can be used. Some BISAC categories also have special keyword requirements on Amazon. Following the tips below will help you avoid punishment by Amazon and can boost your book's placement in Amazon search results.

DO:
- Use Relevant Keywords
- Use Long-Tail Keywords
- Combine Keywords in Logical Order
- Separate Keywords with Commas
- Note Character Limit
- Use 7 Keywords
- Note BISAC Keyword Requirements

DO NOT:
- Variants of Spelling
- Your Title or Author Name
- Other Titles or Author Names
- Subjective Claims of Quality
- Misleading Keywords
- Refer to Temporary Promotion
- Refer to Sales Rank
- Quotation Marks
- Amazon Program Names (KU, KDP)

The most common mistake indie authors make is limiting their seven Amazon keywords to seven actual words. Recent studies show that short-tail keywords, keywords consisting of just one word, do not perform as well as long-tail keywords.

Long-tail keywords are keywords that are made up of multiple words. But these should not be random words lumped together. The keyword phrase should be arranged in logical order. Test your word order by entering words into Amazon's search bar. Amazon's auto-complete will provide popular search word combinations.

Another common mistake is to put your long-tail keywords in quotation marks. Using quotation marks will limit searches to your exact keyword phrase, reducing your book's appearance in search results. Do not use quotation marks, but do separate each keyword or keyword phrase with commas. Commas indicate the break between keywords.

Do not try to increase traffic to your book's product page by being misleading or fraudulent. Relevant keywords will produce the best results and will not risk your page being removed.

There is one more keyword requirement that is extremely important on Amazon. There are keyword prerequisites to being listed in certain categories. The following categories, and all subsequent subcategories, have keyword requirements, including Biographies & Memoirs; Literature & Fiction; Business & Money; Mystery, Thriller, & Suspense; Children's eBooks; Religion & Spirituality; Comics & Graphic Novels; Romance; Erotica; Science Fiction & Fantasy; Health, Fitness, & Dieting; Teen & Young Adult; History; Textbooks; LGBT; and Travel.

Accessing Amazon's category keyword requirements is easy. Go to your **Amazon KDP** account, click **Help**, **Enter Book Information**, and select **Selecting Browse Categories** in the left sidebar. Scroll down and click on your category to get the chart of keyword requirements for listing in that category.

Let's put together what we've learned. Rather than using the short-tail keyword romance, we can use the long-tail keyword romance paranormal shifter. We can change the word order to paranormal romance shifter, since paranormal romance is more logical than romance paranormal. Our keyword is not contained in quotation marks, and is separated from the other six keywords by commas. To be included in the Romance > Paranormal > Werewolves & Shifters category, the words "werewolf" or "shapeshifter" will also need to be used in our keywords.

You are now ready to progress to the next chapter and create your retail product page. Worried about how your keywords will perform? The good news is that Amazon KDP allows you to change your keywords at any time. If you are unhappy with your book's visibility in search results, you can update your keywords. This is a great way to keep up with industry trends and reader preferences.

To update your book's keywords, log in to your **Amazon KDP** account, go to the **Bookshelf** tab, click on the **Edit Button** with three dots beside your book, and select **Edit**

Details. Scroll down to **keywords** and update your book's keywords.

Note that if you are updating keywords on an old book, you may end up with less keywords than you previously had. When I began publishing my books over seven years ago, Amazon KDP had a larger keyword limit and character limit. Changes to those books resulted in having less keywords (the current seven keyword limit), but changing to higher quality keywords still improved book visibility. No matter how old the book, it's never too late to improve its performance.

CHAPTER 11: RETAIL PRODUCT PAGES

Retail product pages are the gateway to your books. The product page is the landing page featuring your book's cover image, description, reviews, and purchase options. Some product pages also provide an author bio and link to more of your books. Knowing how to create and update your product pages is vital to your book's success.

There are many product page pitfalls to avoid, including low quality cover images, grammar mistakes, incorrect or inadequate keywords, and poor formatting. In this chapter, we'll cover the common pitfalls to avoid and easy ways to improve the look and effectiveness of your retail product pages.

DO:
- Quality Book Cover Image
- Include Book Awards
- NYT & USA Today Bestseller
- Enticing Blurb/Description
- Professionally Edit Blurb and Bio
- Quality Author Photo
- Up-To-Date Author Bio
- Editorial Reviews
- Quality Keywords
- Accurate Categories
- Link Print, Ebook, and Audio
- Update and Make Corrections

DO NOT:
- Low Quality Book Cover
- Long Titles
- Title in ALL CAPS
- Mentioning Format in Title
- Spelling Mistakes

- Grammar Mistakes
- Review Quotes in Blurb
- Sale Info in Blurb
- Address/Phone Number
- Review Quotes in Blurb
- False Claims
- Incorrect Series Numbering
- Formatting Mistakes

Release day can be hectic. I highly recommend having your book cover, description, and author bio prepared in advance. It is also helpful to plan your keywords and know your book's categories before publishing your book. Check out the helpful tips below before publishing. Thankfully, if you learn something new in this chapter, you can make changes to books that are already published. Read this chapter's HOW TO for information on how to use Amazon's Author Central, one of the most powerful tools indie authors have for maintaining their book's Amazon product pages. Author Central can help you control product page content and formatting at any time.

BOOK COVER: As we discussed in **Chapter 6: Book Covers**, your book's cover art must be a high quality design and fit your book's genre. In addition to uploading an eye-catching cover, make sure that the file you upload is in high resolution. Low-resolution images will look blurry and will reflect poorly on the overall quality of your book.

SAMPLING: Most retailers will allow readers to read a sample of your book. If you're using a company like Smashwords to distribute to retailers, you will need to select the sampling percentage. The sampling percentage is the percentage of the book that readers can read for free and is calculated from the book's first page. Most authors choose 15-20%. Some retailers will choose their own sampling percentage, usually letting readers read 5-20% for free.

Amazon has its own sampling program, Look Inside. If your Kindle book is published through KPD, your book is automatically enrolled in Look Inside. Adding the Look Inside feature to print books requires publisher enrollment.

Publishers must sign up for this program, agree to Amazon's terms, and certify that they are the rights holder.

TITLE: Do not enter your title in ALL CAPS. Most retailers have restrictions against this practice and will not publish your book if the title is in ALL CAPS. Do not include trademarks, reference other authors, or make claims like "free" or "bestseller" in your book's title.

Lengthy titles are also to be avoided. Studies have shown that readers tend to skim past titles with over 60 characters. Good SEO practice is to keep titles under 50 characters. Words with difficult spellings should also be avoided.

If you've researched your book's keywords, consider working one or two keywords into your title, but do not keyword-stuff your title in a way that does not make sense.

SERIES: If your book is part of a series, provide the series name. Pay attention to how each retailer wants series information. Smashwords has a Series Manager section under Metadata Management where the series name and reading order can be provided. Amazon KDP has a series title field and volume field to be filled out during book publishing. The series title must have fewer than 200 characters, and the volume number must be a whole number and not include any text.

The name of your series can be a good place to insert a keyword, but be careful not to keyword-stuff your series name. For example, I used SEO keywords in the names of my series. My Ivy Granger, Psychic Detective urban fantasy series has the keywords "psychic" and "detective" included. My upcoming Whitechapel Paranormal Society Victorian horror series has the keywords "Whitechapel" and "paranormal" included in the series name.

PUBLISHER: The publisher name is the name you used when acquiring your ISBNs.

DESCRIPTION: This is the information that you'd find on the inside flap of a hardcover or the blurb found on the back of a paperback book. Your description's character limit will depend on the retailer. Amazon requires your description be 30 to 4,000 characters in length. NOOK Press allows up to 5,000 characters. iTunes only allows up to 2,000 characters. Some companies, like Smashwords, ask for a short description of up to 400 characters and a long description up to 4,000 characters.

Like with your book's title, do not enter your book's description in ALL CAPS. Do not include review quotes, false claims (NYT Bestseller, Award Winner), retailer names, addresses, phone numbers, and limited-time promotions.

Write a catchy description that will hook readers. Try to include keywords in the description, but do not list keywords separately below the description or mark with hashtags. Reading the descriptions of successful books in your genre can give you an idea of what works well. If you have difficulty writing your description, hire a copywriting professional. If you do write your own description, have it professionally edited or at least read by several beta readers. If readers find grammatical errors and spelling mistakes in your book's description, they will assume that your book is also filled with errors.

If your book has won awards or reached sales milestones like hitting the NYT bestsellers list, include this with your book's description. You should also add award-winning author and/or NYT bestselling author to your author bio.

ISBN: In most cases you have the choice between using a free ISBN provided by the retailer or POD company, or using an ISBN that you own. Read **Chapter 4: ISBNs and Barcodes** to learn more about ISBNs and how to purchase your own ISBN under your indie publishing name. Remember that a free ISBN will list the retailer or POD company as the publisher on your book's product page. If you want your books to be indistinguishable from traditionally published books, you will need to use your own ISBN.

KEYWORDS AND CATEGORIES: Want to optimize your keywords? Want to include words in your title and description that will help increase your book's visibility? Confused by BISAC codes? Don't miss the tips and tricks provided in **Chapter 10: SEO, Keywords, and BISAC**.

EDITORIAL REVIEWS: Some retailers, like NOOK Press, provide a field for adding editorial reviews during the publishing process. Other retailers, like Amazon, provide an option for adding editorial reviews once the book has been published. We'll cover how to use Amazon's Author Central to add editorial reviews to Amazon product pages once your book goes live.

Editorial reviews should be direct quotes from reliable, professional review sources and must be short in length. Remember to include the review source with the review quote.

CUSTOMER REVIEWS: Customer reviews are different from editorial reviews. Do not quote customer reviews in the editorial review section of your product page. Customer reviews will appear on your product page organically.

Customer reviews are not something that you control in your dashboard or on Author Central, but there are things you can do to increase the number of reviews on your product page. In **Chapter 7: ARCs**, we discussed how to create and distribute advance copies of your book to reviewers. Once your book goes live, reach out to those reviewers and let them know that your book's product page is now online and accepting reviews. Do provide a direct link to your book on all retailers. Do not be pushy or try to bully reviewers into posting a positive review.

On Amazon, you can give well-written, positive reviews a boost. Go to your book's Amazon product page and click on **Customer Reviews** located below the title and author name. You will jump to the **Customer Reviews** section at the bottom of the page. Click the **Number** beside the gold stars to be taken to the dedicated **Customer Reviews** page for your book. You will see the **Top Positive Review** and **Top Critical Review**. One of the factors that makes these "top" reviews is the number of helpful votes they have received. Voting that a review is helpful will give your book and the review a boost. Scroll down to find reviews. There are options for filtering your results. At the bottom of each review there are two buttons. When you find a good review, click the **Yes** button to give Amazon feedback that this is a helpful review.

If a review is particularly nasty (threatens you, your editor, or cover designer as an individual), you can click the **No** button, but use the No button sparingly.

Do not abuse the No button. Do not comment on reviews. Never respond negatively to a review. More information on reviews can be found in the **Super Simple Quick Start Guide to Book Marketing**.

AUTHOR BIO: Write your author bio in third person. Include your accomplishments such as books or series written, awards won, and sales milestones such as becoming a NYT bestseller. If you have many books, series, and accomplishments, stick to the highlights. Your author bio should be concise.

AUTHOR PHOTO: In addition to an author bio, most retailers will allow you to add an author photo. Just like with your book cover, use a professional, high quality image. There are many photographers who do author headshots for a reasonable price. If that is not an option, have a friend take a series of photos of you. Keep your author platform in mind when posing for photos, and include props and settings that relate to what you write. Get a second opinion on what photo to use by posting your top picks to your blog or social networks and let your readers choose their favorite.

CREATING: Once you decide on how to describe and categorize your book, you will need to upload the information for your book's retailers. Some retailers allow you to begin your book's setup before you hit publish. Become familiar with each retailer's author dashboard and consider inputting your book's basic information in advance. If you are setting up a pre-order, keep in mind that the data you provide will appear on the product page from the beginning of the pre-order period. If you intend to make your book immediately available, the information will appear on the book's product page as soon as it goes live.

Your book should begin to appear on retail product pages within 1-3 days for ebooks, but may take up to 6 weeks for expanded distribution of print books. Once you hit publish, there may be a period of hours or days in which you cannot access or make changes to your book's metadata.

UPDATING: If the information on your book's product page is incorrect, do not panic. Your book's data may take hours or days to fully populate the product page. Formatting of your product page can also change. Give the retailer time to fully create your book's product page. I have noticed that print book product pages are notorious for taking days for the book's metadata to fully populate the page.

If you have waited and still see errors, you can go into your dashboard for that retailer or the company you are using to distribute to that retailer (Smashwords, Draft2Digital) and make changes. Changes may take days to appear. If you cannot access your book's metadata, or your changes do not appear after 72 hours, contact customer service. The good news is that you have an additional option when publishing to Amazon.

Amazon has created an author portal giving you control over your product pages. Author Central (authorcentral.amazon.com) is a great tool for updating your book's description, adding professional reviews, and maintaining your Amazon author page. In the tutorial later in this chapter, I'll provide step-by-step instructions on how to customize and update your product pages using Author Central.

LINKING FORMATS: Is your book available in more than one format? If so, you will want to link your product pages. Keeping your book title and series name consistent across channels will help retailers. Going into your Author Central account with Amazon and claiming each book format as yours can also help.

There will still be times that a retailer will not realize that each format is a different edition of the same book. If your book product pages for each format do not link, contact customer service.

For example, you can link your book's print edition and Kindle edition. Go to your **KDP** account, click on the **Help** tab, scroll down, and click on the **Contact Us** button in the left sidebar. Make sure to provide the print edition's ISBN and the Kindle edition's ASIN.

When contacting a retailer's customer service provide as much information as you can. I like to include the book title, author name, ISBN/ASINs, and product page URLs. Make helping you as easy as possible. It may seem like common sense, but be polite in your dealings with retailers. Say please and thank you, and never type your request in ALL CAPS. If you are polite, your customer service representative will be more likely to help you.

HOW TO: Amazon controls 70% of the ebook market and over 60% of the online print market. Your book's Amazon product page can showcase your book in all of its formats (Kindle, print, audio) and link to your author page which showcases you and all of your books, including Kindle, print, audio, and all language translations. This easily makes your book's Amazon product page the most important online real estate that you have.

Author Central is your greatest tool for managing your Amazon product page and author page. You can use your Author Central account to add books to your author page, and add editorial reviews and author bio to your book's product page. You can also add, update, and format your book's description.

Log in to **Author Central** (authorcentral.amazon.com, authorcentral.amazon.co.uk, authorcentral.amazon.de, authorcentral.amazon.fr, or authorcentral.amazon.co.jp). Note that you need an Author Central account for each country's Amazon store. Go to the **Books** tab. Click the **Add More Books** button to claim a book as your own.

PRO TIP: If you can't find your book by its title, try searching by ISBN or ASIN. There is also a common glitch that when you hit save, an error message will say you can't add the book at this time. Click save again. This usually works. If it does not, try again later. New books can take a few days to connect to Author Central.

Once your book is added, it will show in your list of books in the **Books** section of your dashboard and on your Amazon author page. There may be a delay before you are able to access and make changes to your book.

Click on your book. If your book is available on Amazon in multiple formats and you have followed the steps above to have those product pages linked, your book will have each format listed under **Editions** in the top right. Select the edition you want to manage. Audible Audio Editions can be viewed, but updating through Author Central is not supported at this time. Inclusion in the AC dashboard is a positive sign that updating may become available in the near future.

One major difference between your book's Kindle and paperback edition is the dashboard interface for adding and updating editorial reviews.

For print editions, you will need to enter each review quote separately. Go to **Review**, click the **Add** button, enter your review quote and include the review source (mandatory), and click **Save**. A new **Review** field will appear below the first. **Repeat** for each quote.

For Kindle editions, enter all of your editorial review quotes into the same box. Go to **Review**, click the **Add** button, enter all review quotes, and click **Save**.

PRO TIP: Never copy and paste a review from Word or from a website. Author Central is very sensitive and will carry over formatting that will wreak havoc on your book's product page formatting. If you must copy and paste information, paste it into **TextEdit** or use another method to strip the text of all formatting.

The **Description** section is located below the **Review** section. Go to **Product Description** and click the **Edit** button. The **Edit Review** window will open. Note that above and to the right of the text box there is a **Compose** tab and an **Edit HTML** tab. The text in the text box will look differently depending on which tab you are currently viewing.

Click the **Compose** tab (the default) and you will see that there are buttons for Bold, Italics, Numbered List, and Bulleted List. Look at other book descriptions in your genre. You may want to **Bold** your tagline or a sentence that highlights your book's awards and achievements. To do so, **highlight/select** the sentence and click the **Bold** button. Click the **Preview** button. Are the correct words in bold? Is your description's line spacing correct? If not correct, click the **Go Back** button. If you approve, click the **Save Changes** button. Clicking the save changes button is the only way your changes will be made on Amazon.

If you know HTML or are willing to learn the basics, you can click on the **Edit HTML** tab to view the HTML for your book's description. Basic HTML tags are allowed. If you are having trouble with Amazon adding large spaces to your book's description, the **Edit HTML** text box is the best place to fix the problem. Remove the extra **Line Break** tags, click the **Compose** tab, and click the **Preview** button. If not correct, click the **Go Back** button. If you approve, click the **Save Changes** button. Clicking the save changes button is the only way your changes will be made on Amazon.

The sections below your book's **Description (From the Author, From the Inside Flap, From the Back Cover, About the Author**) are optional. Look at product pages for successful books in your book's genre to see how authors and publishers are using these sections.

CHAPTER 12: PRICING

The ability to control book pricing is the strongest leverage we have as indie authors. We can competitively price our books, react instantly to market trends, and use price promotions to boost sales for our books, especially books in a series.

EBOOK PRICING: Indie publishers typically price below traditional publishers. The Big Five publishers continue to see a decline in ebook sales due to their return to agency pricing. If you look at which publishers are earning the most ebook dollars, you'll see that indie authors are making the largest percentage of ebook sales. This is due primarily to low ebook pricing.

Let's look at the numbers. The Big Five's most heavily promoted ebooks are priced in the $11.99 to $14.99 range, and the average ebook price for the Big Five is around $9.50. Most indie ebooks are priced in the $0.00 to $4.99 range, and the average ebook price for indie ebooks is around $2.99.

It is important to note that with indie ebook pricing the strategy is often to provide the first book in a series for free, either temporarily or permafree (meaning it will always be offered for free), or at a reduced price from other books in the series. So while book one might be in the $0.00 to $1.99 range, all other books in the series are often in the $1.99 to $4.99 range.

Ebook pricing is in flux much more than other book formats. During the seven years I've been publishing books, the "sweet spot" price for ebooks has fluctuated wildly. The good news is that most indie books are selling well at a higher price point than in previous years. The current wisdom is to price below the traditional publisher's pricing model, but not to price so low that readers may question your book's value.

Ebook royalties vary depending on the retailer and if you are distributing directly or indirectly to that retailer. It's important to note that your book's Amazon KDP royalty percentage is dependent on your Kindle book's price. Books that are priced below $2.99 or above $9.99 earn a 35% royalty. Books priced $2.99 to $9.99 earn a 70% royalty (dependent on territories). Check the current royalty pricing requirements for each Amazon territory by visiting **Amazon KDP**, **Help**, **Royalty Options**, and click on **List Price Requirements**.

While it is impossible to give a sweeping general recommendation for what your perfect price will be, there are a few tips that can be helpful. Consider royalty rates when trying new price points for your books.

DO:
- Research Genre Specific Pricing Trends
- Experiment with Pricing
- Offer Limited-Time Price Promotions
- Make Book One Less Expensive

PRO TIP: Free ebook pricing will bring a greater quantity of readers, but there are potential pitfalls. Free book downloads will not count toward your ranking on lists for actual sales. Free book downloads can also lead to an increase in bad reviews by readers who tried a book outside their preferred genre.

PRINT BOOK PRICING: Print book pricing is affected by trim size, page count, and print method. Print on Demand companies offer the ability to sell print books with less risk, but you must price high enough to cover the basic print and distribution costs.

Once you calculate your print book's base cost, the price at which you will break even, you need to decide how much or how little profit you are willing to make. The larger the profit margin per book, the higher the cost for the reader. High print book pricing can lead to less actual print book sales. Look at other books in your genre to get an idea of acceptable pricing.

MULTIPLE FORMAT PRICE DEALS: There are various options for offering deals to readers who purchase your book across multiple formats.

Whispersync is a popular way to encourage readers to purchase both the Kindle format and the audio format. We'll discuss how to make your books eligible for Whispersync in **Chapter 13: Audiobooks and Narrators**. Whispersync offers a reduced price deal to readers who purchase your book in both formats. If your books are Whispersync enabled, consider promotions targeting audio and ebook markets.

Similarly, Kindle Matchbook offers readers a reduced price deal when purchasing both the Kindle and print edition of your book. Authors can opt into this program from their book's Amazon KDP page.

If you sell your books directly to readers at events or on your website, you can offer deals when more than one format is purchased together. If selling online, you can offer the deal as a bundle or with a coupon code to be entered in the online shopping cart.

BOOK BUNDLES: You can offer your books in bundles and boxed sets. Ebook boxed sets are increasingly popular. Boxed sets can be books from one author or for multiple authors.

A great way to get exposure for a series is to have the first book in your series available in a multi-author boxed set, but always look at the fine print. You may be giving up your right to adjust pricing for that book for a specified time period, often between six months to one year from the boxed set publication date. Each of these boxed sets will carry a different contract, so make sure to read the fine print closely on the terms of your rights.

PRO TIP: You can set your book pricing for libraries independent of book pricing for retailers. Library pricing can be lower or higher than retail pricing. This is very easy to do, especially if you use Smashwords or Draft2Digital to distribute your books for you. Having your books available in libraries can lend legitimacy to self-published authors who are just starting out, so offering libraries a low price is a good strategy for new authors.

CHAPTER 13:
AUDIOBOOK AND NARRATORS

Audiobooks, also written as audio books, are the fastest growing part of the publishing industry. Audiobooks account for nearly 3 billion dollars in book sales per year, and sales have increased 30-45% in the past two years. Audiobooks can also drive sales to the same book or series in its print and ebook formats. That's a lot of potential dollars in a fast growing market.

So how do you make your book available in audio format? There are four major options to choose from when self-publishing an audiobook. You can hire a production company that covers all aspects of creating your audiobook from casting to final editing, hire a narrator at an agreed upon rate to handle recording and editing with your input, agree to a royalty share in which you and the narrator split royalties, or a hybrid method in which you pay a flat fee upfront and a royalty share at a royalty split more favorable to the author.

- Production Company
- Narrator Hourly Rate
- Narrator Royalty Share
- Hybrid Narrator Rate Plus Royalty

There are pros and cons to each of the above methods. Below we'll cover some of the positives and negatives, and I'll provide tips in the HOW TO section on navigating ACX (Audiobook Exchange) the most popular audiobook creation company for self-publishers.

Unless you hire a production company to handle every aspect of your audiobook, you will need to find a narrator. Finding the right narrator for your book is imperative, but audio narrators are currently in high demand.

Be prepared to spend time searching for your narrator, waiting for auditions, listening to auditions, checking credentials, and negotiating your audio deal. In addition to skill and fit, consider your narrator's following. Research your narrator to see if he/she comes with a built in fan base. It can be worth paying more or waiting longer if your narrator has a large following, so researching their potential impact on sales is worth your time.

Even when you find your perfect narrator and agree on a type of contract, keep in mind that your narrator may not have an opening in their schedule for weeks, months, or years. Be realistic in your audio production timetable, accounting for schedules, narration time, and editing time.

PRO TIP: Discuss release date expectations with your narrator or production company and have a firm completion date in your contract.

Save time by doing some preparation before reaching out to production companies and narrators. If you have not had your book professionally edited, do so now. Errors will be more noticeable when read out loud, and errors to your Kindle book cannot be fixed after your audiobook is produced without risking having Amazon disabling Whispersync. The body of your Kindle book and audiobook must match word for word so that readers can switch seamlessly between both formats.

We discussed audiobook covers in **Chapter 6: Book Covers**. If you haven't created your cover yet, now is a good time. Your book will not be eligible for distribution to retailers without an audiobook cover meeting the requirements of a square 2400 x 2400 pixels image that includes the author name and the title.

If you are planning on trying to entice a high quality narrator into a royalty share deal, you will need to type up a long-term marketing plan. Include plans for promotions, public appearances, and book releases. Provide awards and sales milestones.

No matter what method you use for audiobook creation, I recommend typing up a thorough pronunciation guide. The pronunciation guide should include pronunciations for all character names. A brief summary of each main character, their personality, and story arc is also helpful.

PRODUCTION COMPANY: There are many companies that will handle every aspect of creating your audiobook for you, including BeeAudio, Deyan Audio, Pro Audio Voices, Spoke Media, and VoicesforBooks. This will save you time, but will cost more upfront and you might be left out of some of the decision making.

PAY PER FINISHED HOUR: The narrator charges a set per finished hour rate. The minimum per finished hour rate is $225 (set minimum) for union narrators and around $200 for non union (can fluctuate). There is no maximum, and with the current high demand, skilled narrators can easily cost over $500 per finished hour. The finished hour will depend on book length and read speed.

Let's say we have an 85,000 word book and have agreed to paying $400 per finished hour. If our 85,000 word book comes out to 9 finished hours (this is an example, actual finished hours depend on multiple factors), our audiobook will cost $3,600 plus any additional cost for the audiobook cover.

This method requires paying a large sum upfront, but you retain full control over your work, how and where you sell your audiobook, and you do not split your royalties with the narrator.

ROYALTY SHARE: Royalty share contracts can be done easily through ACX, but it is extremely difficult to find a quality narrator willing to agree to a royalty share deal in today's industry. As recommended above, arm yourself with a marketing plan that demonstrates your willingness to promote the audiobook. Include any awards won or sales milestones achieved. Narrators are going to look at your book's ranking in its current formats, so consider running a promotion to help your rankings.

It's understandable why narrators are hesitant to agree to a royalty share deal. You do not pay the narrator, so the narrator has the most to lose. They risk working for free now in hopes of earning strong royalties later. There is no guarantee that your book will sell and that they will ever see a dime. On the flip side, your audiobook could become a huge success and you will be sharing all of the royalties with your narrator.

With a royalty share, you and the narrator split the royalties (50/50 with ACX), after the retailer or distributor takes their cut. A benefit is that your narrator is relying on the book selling well enough to make money. Royalty share narrators are often motivated and willing to help promote your book post production.

HYBRID: Some narrators are offering a hybrid deal requiring a down payment followed by a royalty share at a lesser rate than a standard royalty share. The down payment amount and royalty percentage can vary wildly.

Note that ACX does not have a hybrid contract, so consider potential legal fees to have your contract drawn up.

HOW TO: ACX has two ready-made author/narrator contracts, one for paying per finished hour and one for a 50/50 royalty share. Read over the contracts before making a final decision about how you create your audiobook. If you decide on one of these contracts, you will need to make your book available for narrators.

ACX (Audiobook Exchange) is an Amazon owned company. Audible is also an Amazon owned company. This connection makes it easy to add your book's information to ACX for audiobook creation and means that your Amazon product page and Audible page will automatically link. It also means that you have a good chance of your book being eligible for Whispersync.

Log in to **ACX** (acx.com) and enter your **Book Title, Author Name, or ISBN** in the search bar. ACX will locate your book on Amazon. **Select** the book you want to create as an audiobook by clicking the **This is My Book** button.

A window will pop up with three options. Click on **I'm looking for someone to narrate and produce my audiobook**. If you have not signed in, you will have to do so now.

Click the **Agree & Continue** button to agree to ACX's policies regarding posting your book and that you are the owner of your book's audio rights.

You will now be able to create a profile for your book. ACX will autofill some fields with information from your book's Amazon page. Make any necessary changes. Remember to entice narrators by mentioning that a marketing plan and pronunciation guide are available upon request.

ACX will require the upload of a short excerpt from your book. This is for potential narrators to read and submit as an audition. I recommend an excerpt that contains some dialogue between your main character and another character that appears often in your book.

You will be able to narrow your search for narrator by providing specific restrictions. Only want a female with a southern accent who sounds between the ages of 25 and 30? Put that in your settings. Being specific will save you, and potential narrators, time and effort.

Some narrators will seek you out from your book's listing, but you can be more proactive. Search the database and reach out to narrators who you think will be a good fit for your book. Narrator profiles usually have samples of their work, a short bio, and a link to their website.

ACX should alert you when your book receives an audition. Make sure your email address is accurate and one you check frequently. Listen to all auditions carefully. When you find your perfect narrator, accept their audition. ACX will provide the contract to digitally sign.

A full manuscript will be required for upload. You will also need to upload the audiobook cover to ACX.

You will need to listen to and approve every individual track from your audiobook before it can be published.

PRO TIP: Ask your narrator if they are willing to upload files to an encrypted file sharing site where you and your narrator can share access to the files. This way you can listen and make editing notes as each chapter is completed, your narrator can make corrections and share the corrected files with you without ever having to wait for a company like ACX to unlock the files. When all edits are done, have the narrator upload the final files, listen one more time, and approve.

DISTRIBUTION: If you agree on a royalty share deal through ACX, your distribution is limited. ACX will handle the distribution for you, which means one account and one royalty payment, but your book will only be sold on Amazon, Audible, and iTunes.

With all other methods, you can choose to distribute direct to retailer, use ACX, or use a company like Author's Republic (authorsrepublic.com) to distribute to multiple retailers, including online stores like AudiobooksNow

(audiobooksnow.com), Audiobooks (audiobook.com), Audiobookstore (audiobookstore.com), and AudioTeka (audioteka.com).

PRO TIP: Be cautious about building reader and blogger expectation for a release date close to the completion date. Once you approve the final files, your book goes into review. This process can take weeks. After the file review stage, your book will enter a production or distribution process that can take additional weeks to complete. With no definite date, it's better to promise a spring or summer release, for example, than a specific release date that could be missed by weeks or even months.

CHAPTER 14:
TRANSLATIONS AND TRANSLATORS

Translations are another important segment of the publishing industry. There has been a decrease in traditionally published translated works in recent years, but the emergence of ebooks, and the growing popularity of, and easy access to, ereaders worldwide mean that there is great potential to reach readers. In fact, the lack of competition makes it easier for your book to get noticed and move up the rankings.

So how do you create a translation of your book? The good news is that self-publishing a translation of your book is similar to producing an audio edition. If you have already published an audiobook, you will be familiar with the basic process, and you will have many of the materials you need to entice quality translators.

There are three major options to choose from when self-publishing a translation of your book. You can hire a translator at an agreed upon rate to translate your book, agree to a royalty share in which you and the translator split royalties, or a hybrid method in which you pay a flat fee upfront and a royalty share at a lower royalty percentage.

- Translator Paid
- Translator Royalty Share
- Hybrid Translator Payment Plus Royalty

There are pros and cons to each of the above methods. Below we'll cover some of the positives and negatives, and I'll provide tips in the HOW TO section on navigating Babelcube (babelcube.com) the most popular translated book creation company for self-publishers.

You will need to find a qualified translator with translation experience, a strong understanding of the origin language, and a strong understanding of the translated language.

Be prepared to spend time searching for your translator, especially if you are shopping your book for a royalty share deal. You will need to set aside time waiting for translation samples, checking samples with readers or colleagues who are fluent in the translated language, checking credentials, and negotiating your translation deal. In addition to their translation skill, consider your translator's following. Does your translator have a built in fan base? Do they have a track record of promoting new translated works to their fans? It can be worth paying more or waiting longer if your translator has a large following, so researching their potential impact on sales is worth your time.

Even when you find the perfect translator and agree on a type of contract, keep in mind that your translator may not have an opening in their schedule for weeks or months. Be realistic in your publishing timetable, accounting for schedules, translation time, and editing time.

PRO TIP: Discuss release date expectations with potential translators and have a firm completion date in your contract.

Save time by doing some preparation before reaching out to translators. If you are planning on trying to entice a high quality narrator into a royalty share deal, you will need to type up a long-term marketing plan. Include plans for promotions, public appearances, and book releases. Provide awards and sales milestones.

You can also save time and begin book promotion early by asking your translator for a few things translated immediately. Ask your translator to translate the title (keep in mind that German law prohibits claiming a title already in use), series name, book description, and author bio. You may also want to ask for sales taglines or promotional statements. Note that, depending on your contract, these translations might cost you an additional fee.

The first thing you should do with these translations is create your ebook cover and begin work on your print book cover. You will need to wait until translation is completed and you have final word count before print cover can be finished, but there is much you can do now. Check and see if your original book cover fonts will support the characters and symbols of the translated language. If not, do not worry. It's not unusual for a German cover, for example, to look different than the English cover. Remember to update the title, series name, and description.

Also consider any potential societal taboos in the cover image. A woman wearing white, for example, is considered pure in American culture, but in many Asian cultures it is similar to a death shroud and represents a period of mourning.

Having the title, series name, book description, author bio, and promo statements translated will allow you to begin promoting before the book's release. You will also be able to add the book to sites like Goodreads (goodreads.com) and create a translated bio for your Amazon author page for your book's target country.

PAID: The translator charges a set rate based on word count. Rates for translators vary, but are often in the $0.06 to $0.15 per word range. In the previous chapter, we used a hypothetical book that was 85,000 words in length. If we are translating that same book into German and our German translator charges $0.10 per word, then the translation will cost $8,500. This is on par with what my German translator charges.

Keep in mind that you may also need to pay an editor who is fluent in that language to check the translation for accuracy. Capturing subtleties and nuances from one language to another takes skill and experience. Consider the need for editing when deciding on a translator and when creating your publishing budget.

This method requires paying a large sum upfront, but you retain full control over your work, how and where you sell your translated book, and you do not split your royalties with the translator.

ROYALTY SHARE: Royalty share contracts can be done easily through companies like Bablecube, or you can write up your own contract. Writing up your own contract has more freedoms, but might incur initial legal fees and requires you to cover the administrative tasks of dealing with retailers and distributors. Also consider how your translator will be paid (PayPal, Check, Bank Transfer), how often they will be paid (monthly, quarterly), and what fees you will be responsible for (PayPal fees, Bank Fees, Postage, Accountant). You will also need to keep impeccable records and provide your translator with periodic sales and royalty reports.

Babelcube charges no upfront fee to the author or the translator, but they do take a percentage (15%) to handle creation, contracts, and distribution. After Babelcube takes their percentage, the remaining royalty is split between the translator and you (the rights holder). The actual percentages depend on your book's cumulative net book royalties. For the first $1,999 the author receives 30% and translator 55%, $2,000 to $4,999 author 45% and translator 40%, $5,000 to $7,999 author 65% and translator 20%, and once the book has earned a net of $8,000 the author earns 75% and the translator earns 10%. Babelcube intentionally weights royalties initially in the translator's favor to cover their costs, since translators are risking the most at the beginning of a royalty share deal.

With a royalty share you and the narrator split the royalties after the retailer or distributor takes their cut. A benefit is that your translator is relying on your book selling well to make money. Royalty share translators are often motivated to create the best product and are willing to help promote your book post release.

HYBRID: Some translators are offering a hybrid deal which requires a down payment followed by a royalty share at a lesser rate than a standard royalty share. The down payment amount and royalty percentage can vary wildly. Note that Babelcube does not have a hybrid contract, so consider potential legal fees, administrative tasks, and payment fees like in the private royalty share deal above.

HOW TO: Babelcube has a ready-made author/translator royalty share contract, handles ebook and print book conversion, distribution, and makes it easy for authors and translators to find each other.

Go to **Babelcube** (babelcube.com). New users need to scroll down to **Authors & Publishers**, and click the **Learn More** button. You can read more about Babelcube by clicking the **Learn How it Works** button, or click the **Translate Your Books** button to get started. You will need to create an account before progressing with your translation. Already have a Babelcube account? Go to Babelcube and click on your name in the upper right.

You will need to create an author profile under the **Profile** tab. Include your author bio, contact information, and social networking links.

Now add the book you are a seeking a translation for. Go to the **Books** tab and click the **Add a New Book** button. Provide your book details in the **Add a Book** window, including **Title, Author, Book Cover** (Original), **One Line Description, Full Description, Genre, Secondary Genre, Book Language (Original), Keywords, Word Count, Book Sales and Rankings, Book Sample Text** (2,000 character max), **Amazon Book Page, Book Website, Facebook Fan Page**, and **Goodreads Book Page**. If your book is already available in certain languages, click **Add Language** under **Translations Status** to let translators know that it is not available for translation in that language. Click the **Add Book** button to save your book's information and create a listing on Babelcube for your book.

Some translators will seek you out from your book's listing, but you can be more proactive. Search the database and reach out to translators who you think will be a good fit for your book. Translator profiles usually have links to their work, a short bio, and a link to their website.

To find translators on Babelcube, go to the **Translators** tab. Select the **Translate From** language and **Translate To** language from the drop down menus. There are also additional options for filtering your search. Click the **Search for Translators** button to see a list of translators who translate according to your specifications.

Babelcube should alert you when your book receives an offer. Make sure your email address is accurate and one you check frequently. When you find your perfect translator, accept their offer. Babelcube will provide the contract to digitally sign.

A full manuscript will be required for upload. You will receive the first 10 translated pages for approval. Read through this carefully. This is the time to catch errors before the translation progresses very far. Have someone fluent in the language, ideally another translator, check the work before approving.

You will need to read and approve the final manuscript before it can be published. When the book is completed you will also need to upload the ebook and print book covers.

PRO TIP: Exchange contact information with your translator. The Babelcube message system is slow. Skype, email, and instant messenger apps can be a great way for your translator to ask questions and get a rapid response.

DISTRIBUTION: If you agree on a royalty share deal through Babelcube, your distribution is limited. Babelcube will handle the distribution for you, which means one account and one royalty payment, but your book will only be sold on partner sites. With all other methods, you can choose to distribute direct to retailer.

At this time, Babelcube distributes to all Amazon stores, Barnes & Noble, Apple iBooks, Kobo, Scribd, and Tolino. They also may distribute to Streetlib, 3M, Baker & Taylor, Follet, Overdrive, Gardners, Chegg, and GooglePlay. Royalty payments are paid directly to the author or translator by Babelcube through PayPal.

PRO TIP: Be cautious about building reader and blogger expectation for a release date close to the completion date. Once you approve the final files, your book will enter a production and distribution process that can take days or weeks.

PRO TIP: Publishing your book in multiple formats and languages is smart business. You've already done the hard work of writing your book, so why not tap into as many revenue streams as possible? Not only will you make more money, but your income is now coming from multiple sources. Just like with diversifying your stock portfolio, if there's a drop in revenue for one outlet, there may be an increase in another outlet. Build financial security by publishing in as many formats and languages as possible.

PUBLISHING CHECKLIST

Being a publisher means running your own business. It is important to stay organized. I use lists to help keep on track with my publishing and marketing tasks. I've compiled a to-do list that may come in handy during your publishing journey.

TO-DO LIST:
- Build a writing template.
- Write a good book.
- Save often.
- Copyright your work.
- Find beta readers.
- Hire an editor.
- Edit draft.
- Purchase ISBNs.
- Collect cover ideas.
- Purchase Fonts.
- Hire a cover artist.
- Compile a list of potential reviewers.
- Format ARCs for ebook.
- Format ARCs for print.
- Order print ARCs.
- Contact reviewers.
- Email or mail ARCs to reviewers.
- Edit final draft.
- Research SEO.
- Choose keywords.
- Select BISAC categories.
- Write blurb/description.
- Create Goodreads book page.
- Add your book to your website.
- Update print cover.
- Enter print info.
- Upload print interior file and cover.

- Order final print proof copies.
- Check proof copies.
- Publish print book.
- Enter info for product pages.
- Upload ebook to retailers.
- Set pricing.
- Select distribution.
- Publish ebooks.
- Update Amazon product page with Author Central.
- Contact reviewers.
- Create an audiobook cover.
- Write a marketing plan.
- Create a pronunciation guide.
- Shop for narrators.
- Listen to auditions.
- Contract for audiobook production.
- Listen and edit audiobook.
- Publish audiobook.
- Shop for translators.
- Read sample translations.
- Contract for translation.
- Read and edit translation.
- Publish translated ebooks.
- Publish translated print book.
- Repeat translations for multiple languages.
- Write next book!

Feel free to customize your checklist. The beauty of self-publishing is that there are few hard rules to follow. Our independence gives us the freedom to try new things and change our publishing strategies as we go. The checklist above is a basic guideline intended as a reminder of tasks to complete and options to consider, taking you one step, leap, and bound closer to successfully publishing your book.

PUBLISHING RESOURCES

Need a quick reference to the helpful publishing resources that we have covered? Visit these online sites to learn more about the topics discussed in this book. For a more comprehensive list of author resources with active, up-to-date links, visit the Resources for Authors page at www.EJStevensAuthor.com.

- ACX
- Amazon KDP
- Apple
- Author Central
- Author's Republic
- Babelcube
- BISAC
- Bowker
- Createspace
- DaFont
- DepositPhotos
- Draft2Digital
- Google AdWords
- IngramSpark
- iStockPhoto
- Kindle Boards
- NOOK Press
- Smashwords
- U.S. Copyright Office

Grab your cape. It's time to be a publishing hero!

WAS THIS BOOK HELPFUL?

Did you find this book helpful? If this book has made your publishing journey easier, please consider writing a review.

Reviews are the single most powerful way to help the book and the author. If you would like to see more Super Simple Quick Start Guides, please leave a review and share with friends and colleagues.

Thank you.

Looking to improve book sales? Check out the Super Simple Quick Start Guide to Book Marketing by E.J. Stevens.

ABOUT THE AUTHOR

E.J. Stevens is the bestselling, award-winning author of the IVY GRANGER, PSYCHIC DETECTIVE urban fantasy series, the SPIRIT GUIDE young adult series, the HUNTERS' GUILD urban fantasy series, and the WHITECHAPEL PARANORMAL SOCIETY Victorian Gothic horror series. She is known for filling pages with quirky characters, bloodsucking vampires, psychotic faeries, and snarky, kick-butt heroines. Her novels are available worldwide in multiple languages.

BTS Red Carpet Award winner for Best Novel, SYAE finalist for Best Paranormal Series, Best Novella, and Best Horror, winner of the PRG Reviewer's Choice Award for Best Paranormal Fantasy Novel, Best Young Adult Paranormal Series, Best Urban Fantasy Novel, and finalist for Best Young Adult Paranormal Novel and Best Urban Fantasy Series.

When E.J. isn't at her writing desk, she enjoys dancing along seaside cliffs, singing in graveyards, and sleeping in faerie circles. E.J. currently resides in a magical forest on the coast of Maine where she finds daily inspiration for her writing. Connect with E.J. on her Website www.EJStevensAuthor.com.

www.ingramcontent.com/pod-product-compliance
Lightning Source LLC
Chambersburg PA
CBHW070648050426
42451CB00008B/309